WALKING ON WATER

Faith and Doubt in the Christian Life

WAYNE BROUWER

CRC Publications
Grand Rapids, Michigan

Library of Congress Cataloging-in-Publication Data
Brouwer, Wayne, 1954-
    Walking on water: faith and doubt in the Christian life / Wayne
Brouwer.
        p.   cm. — (Devotions for today)
    Includes bibliographical references.
    ISBN 1-56212-055-7
    1. Faith. 2. Belief and doubt. 3. Meditations. I. Title. II. Series.
BT774.B76 1994
234'.2—dc20   94-3931
                                                              CIP

10 9 8 7 6 5 4 3 2 1

Contents

Acknowledgments

I don't know you. After you have read this book, you will know me a bit. Maybe we will meet sometime, and we can get to know each other better.

But before you assume that the ideas expressed in these meditations spring solely from my heart and mind, let me recognize a few others who deserve credit for the best that's here.

First, Os Guinness sparked my thinking on questions of faith and doubt with his book *In Two Minds: The Dilemma of Doubt and How to Resolve It* (InterVarsity Press, 1976). If you are familiar with the book, you will soon realize how much I owe him.

Second, I need to thank Harry Emerson Fosdick, gone on to glory, for the insights he brought weekly to his pulpit in New York City a generation ago. Much in these pages is rooted in ideas captured in printed volumes of his sermons.

Third, two congregations deserve a note of appreciation. I first preached a series of sermons on the theme of doubt and faith in the Iron Springs, Alberta, Christian Reformed Church several years ago. More recently, I shared the substance of these meditations in sermons at my present church, First Christian Reformed Church, London, Ontario. Comments of appreciation I received indicated that many were touched by the struggles I have experienced on my pilgrimage of faith.

Finally, I need to thank my family. My wife, Brenda, and our three daughters—Kristyn, Kimberly, and Kaitlyn—shared this journey with me. The hours I spent preparing this manuscript I took from them. I hope the results will make the sacrifice worthwhile.

Some might say that here I should also acknowledge God. I don't think so. I believe the pages that follow are my acknowledgment to him. After all, if I weren't so sure of my need for him and of his love for me, I wouldn't have written about our walk together as a word of encouragement to you.

Wayne Brouwer

Preface

Typically, doubt has had very bad press in Christian circles. It has been viewed as the opposite of faith, as the enemy of faith, as lack of faith. Tennyson reflected a common understanding when he characterized doubt as "devil-born."

But as Miguel De Unamuno wrote,

> Faith which does not doubt is dead faith.

And as Robert Browning wrote,

> You call for faith:
> I show you doubt, to prove that faith exists.
> The more of doubt, the stronger faith, I say,
> If faith o'ercomes doubt.

This book of meditations recognizes the tension between faith and doubt but views them as "Siamese twins." As the author writes, "You can't have faith without doubt trying to unsettle it. And you can't have doubts without faith shouting, 'This far, and no further!'"

The author of these provocative meditations is Wayne Brouwer, pastor of the First Christian Reformed Church of London, Ontario. He has written numerous articles and meditations in *The Banner*, in *Christian Courier*, and in *Reformed Worship*.

We offer these meditations for adults on doubt and faith with the prayer that they will strengthen your faith.

Harvey A. Smit
Editor in Chief
Education Department
CRC Publications

Week 1
Faith and Doubt—
Siamese Twins

The term *Siamese twins* was coined in the nineteenth century when Chang and Eng were born in Siam, now known as Thailand. The brothers spent their whole lives joined from breastbone to navel. Chang and Eng became famous as circus celebrities but also managed to have rather normal lives. Both married and fathered several children. They lived a full life, dying together in 1874 at age 63.

The fascinating thing about Siamese twins (more correctly called conjoined twins) is their extremely close bond. Conjoined twins spend all their waking and sleeping hours together. Often they share organs, and certainly they know each other more intimately than any other two persons could.

Not too different, really, is the relationship between faith and doubt in the Christian's life. I've often wondered about the fact that Jesus' disciple Thomas is called a twin. Probably he had a brother the same age. But the twinning of his believing and doubting spirit makes him our twin as well.

"I Doubt It!"

Read Psalm 14

The fool says in his heart, "There is no God!"
—Psalm 14:1

In her book *A Man Called Peter*, Catherine Marshall tells the tale of her larger-than-life husband. Among other things, she says, he was a "GGP"—a "Great Games Player." He loved to have friends over for an evening of game playing, the more competitive the better. Only a rare expression of cunning enabled someone else to defeat "Peter the Great." The GGP nearly always came out on top.

My daughters think I'm a GGP, too. I love games. I revel in the competition and play to win. My competitive spirit might simply be a part of my character, or it might have grown from my need, as a youngster, to hold my own against my sisters. We grew up playing Scrabble, chess, checkers, and all kinds of other games.

As children, one of our favorites was the card game "I Doubt It!" After the deck was dealt, we took turns laying a card face down, one by one, on a pile in the center of the table. Whoever started named the color each time around. If she said hers was red, we would each shout "red!" as we slapped our card down. If she said "black!" we'd each declare the card we laid black as well.

The object was to be the first to get rid of all your cards. Here was the catch: the other players could challenge you whenever they wanted by saying, "I doubt it!" Then you'd have to reveal the last card you played. If the required color was red but you played a black card, you had to pick up the whole pile.

We all doubted each other, of course. It was the name of the game. Sometimes our doubts were accurate, sometimes they proved false—and not without consequences. If I said, "I doubt it" when someone laid a card, but she was telling the truth, I'd have to add the whole pile to my hand.

Doubt and faith were just a game to us then. Of course we believed everything our parents told us. Of course we believed everything we heard at church. Of course we believed in God and the Bible and Jesus Christ.

None of us dared to say "I doubt it" when the truths of Christianity were on the table. We never even considered it.

That's why when we were young, Thomas was always the bad guy in our minds. He was almost as bad as Judas, you know. Judas may have killed Jesus with his actions, but Thomas killed Jesus again in his heart. He doubted! For a whole week after Easter he didn't believe. He wouldn't believe. He refused to believe.

Doubting Thomas. The name was like a black cloud on a sunny day. For us, faith was faith, and it left no room for doubt.

∽

Lord, help us not to be fools who say in our hearts that you don't exist. Keep us from playing games in life that deny what you have told us is true. Let our faith go beyond childish innocence to deeper devotion. In Christ, Amen.

Questions

Read Psalm 73:1-14

Surely in vain have I kept my heart pure.
—*Psalm 73:13*

It wasn't until I went away to college that I began to appreciate doubting Thomas for who he really was. Several things brought about that change in me. For one thing, my best friend from high school lost his faith.

He didn't lose it all at once; it happened in stages, bit by bit. First, his sister was killed in a violent accident. She was working that summer on a highway construction crew. She held the flags, signaling traffic to stop or slow down. One morning a pickup truck roared down the highway without slowing down. It slammed into her, killing her instantly.

My friend asked why. Why just then in her life, when she was so young, so full of enthusiasm, so godly? If anyone deserved to live, it was she! Why did she have to die, and in such a violent way?

That's when the doubts first attacked. That's when my friend started losing his faith. And I didn't know what to do. In my heart I was asking the same questions, but I wouldn't admit it openly. Isn't it a sin to question God? Isn't doubt the worst thing that can enter your mind?

But my friend's journey with doubt was only beginning. At college we both majored in philosophy. The questions we discussed in class challenged our faith. Then my friend wrote a paper expressing more doubts than I would have ever dared. He questioned some of the basic beliefs of the church. He challenged the theological "proofs" that didn't prove anything. Again I didn't know how to react.

One summer my friend accompanied a missionary to Mexico. As the missionary brought the message of the gospel to students on university campuses, my friend circulated at the fringe of the crowds, listening to the biting talk of Communist guerrillas. Their outlook captivated him. The next year he went to Italy to follow the footsteps of the Red Brigade, the most violent revolutionary organization in the world during the 1970s.

Eventually my friend tired of that way of life and returned to North America. But he wasn't ready to come back to church or our home community. The politeness of small-town faith left him an exile and a foreigner.

As I watched his faith slip away, I was troubled. It bothered me that he left the church and gave up his Christian faith. What bothered me even more was the realization that his thinking was so clear, that his views about the church, the Bible, and God seemed so right. Most of all, I was troubled that I couldn't provide answers that would change his heart or mind—and that I didn't really want to. Inside, I knew he was more honest than I was. If I brought him back, I'd only be denying the truth of his words.

I was more confused than ever.

~

In the struggles of our lives, Lord, help us to be honest.
Keep us from sugarcoating our faith with trite expressions
that lack meaning. Keep our hearts from denying the
questions that challenge us or the mysteries that unsettle us.
All we ask is that you see us through. Amen.

Freedom

Read Galatians 3:26–4:7; 5:1

It is for freedom that Christ has set us free.
—Galatians 5:1

As I watched my friend's faith slip away, I began to lose my footing. I wasn't as open about it as he, but in real ways, I lost my faith too.

I remember reading the novel *Of Human Bondage* by Somerset Maugham. It is the story of a young Englishman named Philip Carey who was orphaned early in life and adopted by his uncle and aunt. His uncle, the strict pastor of a small congregation, took acts of religious devotion very seriously. Sometimes Philip found his uncle's religious teachings oppressive; yet he never thought of challenging his uncle's faith or questioning his own.

Then, on a trip to Germany, Philip met an American student named Weeks. Weeks challenged Philip's faith, questioned his motives, and demanded that he think about *why* he believed as well as *what* he believed. After a while, Philip's defenses crumbled, and he gave up his Christian faith.

Everyone who knows Somerset Maugham knows that Philip's story is the tale of his own life. This is what happened to him. In one of the book's most powerful passages, Maugham shows Philip standing on a high hill, looking out at the nighttime world. Excitement swells within him as he senses his new freedom: "There is no God! The church doesn't have a hold on me! I am master of my own life!" Says Maugham, "When Philip ceased to believe in Christianity he felt that a great weight was taken from his shoulders."

The day I read those words, I gave up my faith in God.

Doubting Thomas. Doubting friend. Doubting Philip. For me, these were the holy Trinity. These were the honest souls in my world. These were the truly good guys, who had the courage to stand against the simpleminded faith of the masses.

Doubting Thomas. Doubting friend. Doubting Philip. And now, doubting Wayne. It was an exhilarating moment of freedom.

Dr. Leslie Weatherhead, a Christian pastor and psychiatric counselor, summarized his perceptions of humankind in a book called *The Christian*

Agnostic. "I have always been attracted," he writes, "by those lovable men and women who rarely have anything to do with organized churches but who would never act dishonorably or meanly, who are full of generosity and helpfulness if ever one is in trouble or need, who bear their own troubles with magnificent courage, who never complain or grumble or gossip or run other people down." He goes on to say that, for some, organized religion is the very thing that stands in the way of faith.

I know what he means. Religion that leaves no room for doubt robs faith of its vitality. Any god who cannot understand the emotional and psychological questions in the creature he made must be the cruelest divinity every foisted upon humankind. Something within us cries for the freedom to disbelieve, if for no other reason than that faith which is coerced is no faith at all.

∼

God of freedom, help us find our wings. Help us take to flight, not burdened artificially by religious trappings that violate what you have made us to be. Help us doubt with courage, but not with carelessness. And let our doubts lead us to ground that is firmer than rule or coercion or force. In the freedom of Christ we ask it. Amen.

Everybody Doubts

Read Luke 24:36–43

They still did not believe it.
—*Luke 24:41*

Once my faith was shaken, I adopted a new attitude. I thought I was unique at a Christian college, the only doubter on campus. I thought I was one of the few truly honest people in the world. Others around me, I was sure, lived by these lines from the evangelist Thomas Baird:

> Is there no knowledge to be had?
> Has God not spoken once for all?
> Indeed He has; all doubt is mad,
> And destined to disastrous fall.
>
> For God is God, and truth is true,
> All doubt is sinful in His sight;
> And doubters will have cause to rue
> Their doubts through Hell's undoubted night.

But then I started listening to the deeper talk of those around me who called themselves Christians. My classmate whose father committed suicide. A girlfriend whose bright, sunny daytime faith turned into nightmares of doubt in the evening darkness. A retired couple who had given their lives to the church and were left wondering why.

I remember reading one day in Luke's gospel that *all* of Jesus' disciples doubted him after his resurrection. This brought me up short. Wasn't their doubt as big as that of Thomas? Could they point a finger at him without pointing four others back at themselves?

I realized then that to believe in God is not easy. People doubt the story of the resurrection every day. Challenging faith when life turns harsh is about as common as questioning the integrity of politicians! Who hasn't done it? And who won't do it tomorrow?

For doubt is possible only because of our capacity to believe. Doubt demands that we believe only what is true and right and important. Doubt says that I can choose to believe or not believe. Doubt separates me from animals. Animals live by instinct, by learned patterns of behavior, by the commands of the seasons. But I can doubt my feelings, my knowledge, and my instincts. I am able, even, to change my beliefs.

Everyone doubts God. Even the greatest man or woman of faith doubts. Listen to Gideon, chosen by God as a leader of ancient Israel: "If the LORD is with us, why has all this happened to us?" (Judg. 6:13). Is that a shout of faith? Isn't it more the lament of doubt?

David cries out, "How long, O LORD? Will you forget me forever?" (Ps. 13:1) The Sons of Korah complain, "My tears have been my food day and night, while men say to me all day long, 'Where is your God?'" (Ps. 42:3) Asaph, the temple choir director, who constantly gave himself to magnificent services of worship, actually denies his faith (Ps. 73). And Job trembles in agony when he says, "I cry out to you, O God, but you do not answer" (Job 30:20).

Even our Lord struggled with doubts. What do we read about his struggles in Gethsemene, his misgivings, his inner conflicts, the clash between his personal desires and the path he knew he had to take? Have you ever sweat the blood right out of your forehead? Have you ever doubted your faith so much?

Think about Jesus' words from the cross. Hanging helpless, nails tearing his flesh, muscles in agony, death slowly taking hold, what words came to him, this man trained in the Hebrew Scriptures?

They are the words of David in Psalm 22: "My God, my God, why have you forsaken me?"

Is that a cry of faith? Certainly not. Has doubt ever spoken more loudly?

Everybody doubts. It's part of being human, part of what it means to be thinking and choosing and believing creatures. If we are able to have faith, doubt comes with the territory.

~

Creator God, thank you for the strange intricacy of our
thinking and willing and doing. Help us to be gentle with
those who doubt us, for we ourselves have doubted others
along the way. And treat us patiently in our doubts
about you, for the struggles of faith often draw
from us questions and uncertainty. Amen.

Everybody Believes

Read Acts 17:16-28

*Men would seek him and perhaps reach out for him and find
him, though he is not far from each one of us.*
—*Acts 17:27*

If we can be certain of this one thing—that everybody doubts God and
the teachings of Christianity at one time or another—we can also be certain that everyone also believes sometimes. If there is doubt in every
human heart, there is also faith.

Remember the tale of Philip Carey, the hero of Somerset Maugham's
novel *Of Human Bondage?* As he stood on the hillside the night he
rejected Christianity, he breathed in the air of his newfound freedom. "He
was free," says Maugham, "from degrading fears and free from prejudice.
He could go his way without the intolerable dread of hell-fire. He could
breathe more freely in a lighter air."

So what is the first thing Philip did in the rush of his excitement?
What was his first thought, his first inclination, his first activity of freedom? "Unconsciously," says Maugham, "he thanked God that he no
longer believed in Him."

Can you see it? Maybe we lose our faith in God. Maybe we lose our relationship with the church. Maybe we lose our hold on the doctrines we
were taught. But we can't stop believing, can we? Thomas doubted, but
there were things that he still held to. "I trust my eyes," he said. "I believe
what my fingers can touch. I have faith in what I can hear with my ears."

None of us can live as complete skeptics. We believe in love. Or we believe in life. Or we believe in ourselves. We have to cling to something, or
we cease being human altogether.

I had a friend who always wore long-sleeved blouses to cover the scars
on her wrists. Years before, when her doubts had finally taken over, she
put a razor blade to her veins and tried to take her life. After all, she said,
she wasn't human anymore, because she had nothing to believe in: not
God, not friends, not even herself. When the doubts took over, when her
faith was entirely gone, she ceased being a living person. And there she lay
in a bathtub of hot water and blood, until someone carried her to the hospital and forced her to start living again, against her doubting will.

Maybe you doubt God today. Maybe you are more similar to Thomas than to the other disciples. Maybe you're more honest than your parents were about the struggles of faith. But hang onto this thought: you also believe!

Thomas couldn't believe that Jesus was alive, but there were elements of his faith that couldn't be shaken. The great skeptic David Hume might have formed his creed this way: "I doubt, therefore I am." But he was no more in touch with life than was the great theologian Augustine, who shouted, "I believe, and therefore I am!"

Where do you stand? Probably, along with me and five billion other people, you are balancing on the line between doubt and faith. After all, you're only human.

~

Father of Jesus, lead me in the path of faith like a child. I cannot live without faith, and I cannot live apart from doubt. All I ask of you is that you will help me to know the certainties of life that will keep me in tune with eternity. In Christ, Amen.

Circling Our "Think"

Read Mark 9:2-24

"I do believe; help me overcome my unbelief!"
—Mark 9:24

The two truths we need to know today are that we all doubt and we all believe. Faith and doubt live in our hearts like Siamese twins. You can't have faith without doubt trying to unsettle it. And you can't have doubts without faith shouting, "This far, and no further!"

A man watched a little girl draw pictures. He asked her how she did it—how she made her pictures. She said, "First I think, and then I draw a line around my think!" Isn't that a beautiful way to put it?

That's how faith and doubt work in our lives. First we think, like Thomas did, and then we "draw a circle around our think." Whatever is inside the circle is our faith, and whatever is outside is our doubt. A living Jesus, Thomas tells his friends, may be inside your circle of think, but he's outside mine.

But here's the interesting part: the lines of our "think" keep moving. Much of the excitement in life is found in drawing and redrawing the lines around our "think."

A skeptical medical student once told a pastor about his work with cadavers. "I've dissected dozens of human bodies," he said, "but I haven't yet found a soul."

Was the pastor's faith shaken? Of course not. He said to the student, "Tell me more. When you dissected a brain, did you find a thought? When you opened up a heart, did love spill out? When you looked into an eye, could you see a vision?"

The student's problem isn't his scalpel but his "think" and the lines he draws around it. His faith needs to take on more territory, and his doubt needs to give way. Faith and doubt will always live together in his soul, but the line between them will always be changing.

That's what happened to Thomas. In fact, that's what happened to all of the disciples at one time or another. Perhaps no one has caught the tension between faith and doubt better than the painter Raphael. In his masterpiece based on the Transfiguration, he pictures Jesus in all of the splendor of his divinity. Peter, James, and John are roused with ecstacy as

Moses and Elijah descend from heaven to the mountain. Peter wants them to stay there forever in the strength of great faith.

But at the bottom of the painting, down in the shadows beneath the mountain, Raphael pictures a father and son. The boy is epileptic. He keeps tripping into the fire and falling into the water, endangering his life.

The disciples who are nearby can't help him, and the colors of his world are black. When Jesus comes down the mountain, the boy runs to him as if to say, "I believe, but help me with my doubts!" In a sense he's asking Jesus to show him how to retrace the lines of his "think." He's asking for a firmer grasp on his faith and a way to push back the dark edges of doubt.

As we study the scene, the boy becomes the focus of our gaze. And maybe, if we're honest with ourselves, we'll admit that his prayer echoes in our hearts as well.

~

Jesus, there are times when we see the brightness of your glory and power and divinity as clearly as Peter, James, and John did on the mountain. But many times we live with the father and his son down in the dark corners. Today we pray the prayer that resonates in our hearts: "We believe! Help us now with our doubts!" Amen.

Working with the Tools of Doubt

Read John 11:1-16; 14:1-7; 20:24-31

Thomas said to him, "My Lord and my God!"
—John 20:28

How do we make our doubts work for us in the midst of life's struggles? Doubting Thomas may have something to teach us. We find him at center stage on several important occasions in the gospel of John.

In chapter 11, when Jesus tells his disciples he has to go to Jerusalem, Thomas is the first to speak. He says, "Let's go with him and die with him there!" He's not a doubter on that occasion—he doesn't even waver.

John 14 paints a similar picture of Thomas. Jesus tells his disciples that he has to leave them for a time. He says they already know where he's going. But Thomas has no clue about what Jesus is saying. So he in effect blurts out, "Where are you going, Lord? I don't know what you're talking about!"

That's not doubt; that's honesty. Honesty is what characterizes Thomas, not mere doubt. Thomas is like a little boy in elementary school who raises his hand and says, "Teacher, I don't get it!"

For Thomas, doubt and faith work hand in hand. Because his doubt challenges his faith, his faith becomes stronger. His faith gains clarity—he knows exactly what it takes for him to believe something. It gains conviction—you hear this when he finally cries out, "My Lord and my God!" That's not a question or a wish; it's the conviction of great faith.

Because of his doubts, Thomas' faith also gains comfort. The early church claimed that Thomas went to India to bring the message of Jesus, risen from the dead. That's an extremely hard message for a Hindu society to accept. And yet, to this day, a group of churches scattered throughout India calls itself the "Mar Thoma Church." For generations these people have believed in Jesus because of the testimony of Thomas. Not Thomas the saint, but Thomas the doubter. Thomas the questioner. Thomas the honest.

When Thomas finally spoke about Jesus, he was certain. Doubt had clarified his faith, had given him a sure conviction, and had confirmed for him the true source of his comfort. Here was a man of faith. And he got there on the wings of doubt.

Do you believe in God? If you don't, I can certainly understand, for I'm your brother in doubt, and my pilgrimage has led me through the territory you are going through.

But if you are struggling, let your doubt work with your faith! Go ahead and question your faith. Move the lines that you've drawn around your faith. But do it with the honesty of Thomas. And when the lines are drawn again, you'll know the clarity, conviction, and comfort of your faith.

It may not happen all at once. It didn't for me. And it won't bring you entirely beyond the struggles of your soul. I know that all too well.

But this I also know: your struggles will point you to the future instead of the past and will give you this song to sing:

> Oh yesterday our little troupe was ridden through and through,
> Our swaying, tattered pennons fled, a broken, beaten few,
> And all the summer afternoon they hunted us and slew;
> But tomorrow, by the living God, we'll try the game anew!

For the game is the game of life. And our doubts march with us along the way. But deep inside, God has planted the seed of faith, and tomorrow we'll feel it grow strong again!

❧

God of grace, nurture the seed of faith that you've put in our hearts. Help us to know that we belong to you and that even when we're not sure of ourselves we're never beyond your love and care. Give us the honesty of Thomas to make our doubts work hand in hand with our faith. In Christ, Amen.

Week 2
A Room Called Remember

Every school year, each of our daughters is the celebrated student in her class for a week. Her picture is posted prominently. She gets to lead the class in routine exercises. Her life's story is retold in pictures she brings from home.

In our game room closet, we have a large box bulging with family pictures. The box is our treasure chest of memories, cracked and fading, frozen in time. Each year when our girls come calling for pictures, we take a journey into that special little room, not too tidy but full of treasures. It's our room called Remember!

Dreams

Read Genesis 28:10-21

*He had a dream in which he saw a stairway resting on
the earth, with its top reaching to heaven.*
—*Genesis 28:12*

If you have ever heard a violinist perform Giuseppe Tartini's "Devil's
Trill Sonata," you've heard a spectacular piece of music. Few violin com-
positions work the fingers and bow as quickly.

The story behind the "Devil's Trill Sonata" is as fascinating as the com-
position itself. One night, Tartini had a vision so vivid that to his dying
day he wasn't sure whether it had been a dream or something more. He
dreamed that while he was practicing his violin, the devil appeared. After
a time, Tartini handed his violin to the devil, asking him to play. The
devil played a solo so powerful, so magnificent, that Tartini was overwhelmed.

Just as the devil finished, the sleeping Tartini awoke. While the dream
still echoed in his mind, he grabbed his violin, in hopes of remembering
what he had heard. He named the resulting piece of music for the one
who had inspired it.

Some dreams are like that—so real and gripping that we are left wondering whether the dreamworld is actually reality. The ancient Chinese
philosopher Chuang Tzu once dreamed he was a butterfly. When he
awoke to see his human form, he was curious: was he perhaps truly a butterfly dreaming he was a man, or was he a man who sometimes dreamed
he was a butterfly? Could one reality be proved over against the other?

The poet Stephen Vincent Benét wrote that "dreaming men are
haunted men." So it would seem throughout the Scriptures: Jacob was so
haunted by his dream at Bethel that his whole outlook on life was
changed. Nebuchadnezzar may have been able to conquer the world, but
the dreams that robbed him of sleep in Babylon's palace also robbed him
of his kingdom. Or think of Paul in the New Testament. His dreamlike
vision of the Macedonian man launched the mission of the early church
into the far reaches of Europe.

Researchers say we all dream, for better or for worse. In fact, we can't survive without some "dream-sleep" each night. That doesn't mean we all remember our dreams. Those who do may be the lucky ones.

Sometimes our dreams are desperate nightmares. You know the kind: we're choking or falling or standing in front of a crowd without any clothes on (that's the one we preachers get on Saturday nights when our sermons aren't what they should be).

Sometimes our dreams are funny. When I was growing up, I used to wake my family late at night, upstairs in our farmhouse, by laughing and laughing at dreams I'd had. I don't remember what the dreams were about, but my sisters didn't think they were at all funny at the time.

But other dreams—dreams like Tartini had, like Jacob had, like John had on the island of Patmos—can change our lives. They can give us new perspectives and help us better understand our purpose on earth. Our dreamworld may be our closest link with the spiritual world. Some who listen closely at night might hear, with Tartini, the devil's trill; some might find, with Jacob, that they're tenting on holy ground.

~

*God of the night and the day, help us to understand your
conversations with us, whether they shout to us from the
pages of Scripture or whisper to us in the nighttime quiet of
our resting minds. Let us be haunted by your presence,
for in your presence we find ourselves. Amen.*

Homecoming

Read Revelation 21:1–4

He will wipe every tear from their eyes.
—Revelation 21:4

The Christian author Frederick Buechner once wrote about a dream he'd had in which he was staying at a hotel with hundreds of rooms. When he checked in, the desk clerk gave him the key to a delightful room. It made him feel warm, comfortable, and cared for. Although later Buechner couldn't remember exactly what the room looked like, he shivered with pleasure whenever he thought about it.

In his dream, he stayed in the room for a short time before setting off on a number of adventures. Later, however, his dream brought him back to the same hotel.

This time the clerk gave Buechner the key to a different room. When he opened the door, he immediately sensed the difference: it felt cold and clammy; it was cramped and dark; it made him shudder with fear.

So, in his dream, he went to the front desk and asked the clerk to move him to his first room—the bright and cozy one. But Buechner couldn't remember where it was.

The clerk smiled and said he knew exactly which room it was. He told Buechner he could have the room any time he wanted it—if he asked for it by name. The name of the room, said the clerk, was Remember. A room called Remember.

That's when Buechner woke up. And he has been haunted by that dream ever since. A room called Remember! A room of peace. A room that made him feel loved and at home.

What was it all about? Buechner knew. We all have memories, he said—bits and pieces of things that have happened to us in the past; scraps of stories and songs we've learned; photo albums of our younger years. We all remember.

But, said Buechner, we don't always use our memories. Sometimes we let them go to waste. Sometimes we shut them out of our consciousness. Sometimes we're too busy to visit with them. And when we stop using our memories, we lose an important part of our lives.

Throughout the Scriptures we hear God calling us to remember: Remember what life is about. Remember who I am. Remember what you've gone through. Remember who you are.

One of the most powerful scenes in the Bible pictures Jesus calling us to remember. On the night of his death, Jesus sits quietly with the twelve, raises the cup in blessing, and says, "Whenever you come together, do this and remember me."

A father watched proudly as his radiant daughter stood waiting to go on her first date. She was excited and nervous, and so was he. What advice could he give her without being overprotective? He put his arm around her shoulder and looked her lovingly in the eye. "Remember who you are," he said. And that was enough.

∾

Lord our God, help us to find our treasure house of memories. Help us to stock the room with events and ideas and images that are good and right and noble. Help us to return often to recover our sense of self. And always, when we get there, let us know that we are coming home to you. In Christ, who calls us to remember, Amen.

Stocking the Storehouse

Read Numbers 15:37–41

Then you will remember.
—Numbers 15:40

Have you ever seen a devout Jew wearing a prayer shawl like the one described in Numbers 15? The ends of it hang below the hem of his coat, tassels swinging as he walks. If you stand close enough, you might see a single blue thread almost hidden among the others.

What's the point of a prayer shawl? Nobody needs one in order to pray. I doubt, even, that God would expect the Jewish people to wear a shawl in all times and circumstances. The point is not necessity but opportunity. Now and then we need to be confronted by things that will jog our memories and remind us of who we are.

Perhaps you remember playing "Ring around the Rosie" when you were younger. Holding hands with other children, you danced in a circle and chanted,

> Ring around the rosie,
> A pocket full of posies,
> Ashes! Ashes!
> We all fall down!

When you sang the last line, you all tumbled to the ground.

Most kindergartners still play that game. But do you know where it began? In the fourteenth century, the bubonic plague gripped Europe, killing over half the population. Children in England created this game because it mirrored the world in which they lived.

When a person was infected with the plague, the first indication was a dark ring surrounding a bright red spot on the skin—a ring around the rosie. To cover the stench of death, people stuffed their pockets with sweet-smelling posies. And since not all of the corpses could be buried, great piles of human bodies were burned in the open fields—Ashes! Ashes! Before long, those who had disposed of the remains of others died themselves—All fall down!

Every time the children played this game they were remembering who they were. They were telling about their life.

Sometimes our memories are filled with scenes of death, disease, and disaster. We begin to think we are victims and leftovers.

But it doesn't have to be this way. If we are wise, we learn to keep other memories in our hearts as well. God instructed Moses to make sure the Israelites stored many items in their memory closets: divine teachings, covenant love, and the sweet smell of freedom from slavery.

Then, said God, when my people go back to the treasure house of their soul, they'll remember who they are and sing songs of deliverance.

~

Teach us early in life, Lord, to find the good in our
circumstances and to store the beautiful in our minds.
Help us not to ignore or deny the evil that surrounds us.
Remind us often that we can find ourselves in your love.
Through Christ we pray. Amen.

The Tragedy of Forgetfulness

Read Psalm 106

They forgot the God who saved them.
—*Psalm 106:21*

One of the saddest human experiences is the loss of memory. In an article in *The New York Review of Books* (February 16, 1984), Oliver Sacks tells the tragic story of a man's ordeal with Korsakov's syndrome, a disease that attacks the sections of the brain that store memories. The disease wipes the slate clean; all the things you've done, all the people you've known—spouse, children, friends—are suddenly gone.

In his article, Sacks quoted Spanish filmmaker Luis Buñuel, who watched his mother lose her memory over a decade. She forgot even the simplest things in life, like how to tie her shoes and where she had grown up. Worse still, she forgot her own son. She could no longer function in society; when her memory left, so did her identity. "Memory is what makes our lives," said Buñuel. "Life without memory is no life at all." Reflecting on his own life, he said, "Our memory is our coherence, our reason, our feeling, even our action. Without it, we are nothing." When his mother finally died, he considered it a blessing.

If memory is an important part of our human identity, it also plays a critical role in our spiritual identity. When we forget the past, our relationship with God is threatened. Psalm 106 is a terrifying tribute to that reality. It is a litany of lost peoples, a lament tracing the disintegration of the nation of Israel. The Israelites forgot the past, says the psalmist. They forgot the commandments of God. They forgot to go back to the room called Remember.

And when they forgot, they died. They lost their identity as a people. In truth, they ceased to exist.

Charles Dickens wrote a story called *The Haunted Man*. It is the tale of a chemist who wants to be free from his troubling memories. He wants a fresh start in life, unhindered by the ghosts of the past.

Miraculously, he is given the ability to forget. He wipes out the past, locks the door on the room called Remember. But as his memory vanishes, he learns an immortal truth: Losing his memory is the worst curse he could bear. As the story concludes, the man cries out, "Lord, keep my memory green!"

We all need to bring that request to heaven's gates more often, because if we lose our memory, we lose our very selves.

~

Lord, keep my memory green! Help me to remember who I am because of what you have done in my life. Teach me afresh the stories of my past and the journeys of my spirit. Revive in me the knowledge that you have formed me, fashioned me, and made me what I am today. Lord, keep my memory green! Amen.

Back to the Future

Read 1 Chronicles 16:1-2, 7-36

Remember . . . from everlasting to everlasting.
—1 Chronicles 16:12, 36

At the start of his brilliant reign as king of Israel, David casts a deliberate eye to the past. He brings the ark into his capital, Jerusalem, calling attention to its significance for the nation. In a sense, the ark is for Israel a room called Remember. It's a reminder that God is the real King on this throne; it's a traveling storybook of the nation's history.

David knows that the only way to the future is through the doorway of the past. "Remember!" he says to the crowds. "Remember the wonders God has done. Remember the miracles. Remember the way God created and formed us and guided us along through life. Remember!"

David's challenge is for all of us. We find our future when we reap the harvest of our memory. Read this story, and you will discover what I mean.

A. J. Cronin was a doctor who worked in England in the 1920s. In his autobiography, *Adventures in Two Worlds*, he describes working in the hospital of a poor northern mining district early in his career.

One evening a boy dying of diphtheria was brought to him. The hospital was dirty and poorly equipped, with no trained help. Still, Cronin had no alternative but to cut a hole in the boy's throat and insert a breathing tube in his windpipe. Only this emergency tracheotomy saved the fellow's life.

Exhausted, Dr. Cronin left the room. He called a young nurse to sit by the bed. She was only a wisp of a girl, and half starved, but she was a nurse, and she would have to do. "Make sure the tube stays clear, and don't take your eyes off him," he told her. Then he lay down in a corner and slept.

Suddenly the young nurse was shaking him. She had fallen asleep too, and the tube had shifted. The boy had suffocated; he was dead.

Dr. Cronin's eyes blazed in anger. He told her that he would report her, that she'd never work as a nurse again. Standing in front of him, frail, timid, and shaking like a leaf, she mumbled something under her breath. "What's that you're saying?" he demanded.

So she said it a little louder: "Please give me another chance!" But he was furious that she dared ask such a thing. "You're finished," he said. "There will be no more chances for you!"

He stormed away and tried to sleep. But sleep wouldn't come because her words echoed through his mind: "Give me another chance. Please. Give me another chance!"

In the morning he tried to write the letter of discipline, but the picture of her pleading face wouldn't leave him. Finally he tore the letter up.

But that's not the end of the story. That poor, feeble creature, more child than woman, went on to become the matron of one of England's greatest children's hospitals. In her later years, she was known throughout the nation for her wisdom and devotion.

Do you understand what happened? Do you know what made her such a great woman? It was her room called Remember. She never forgot what happened that night. She never forgot her failure. And she never forgot the grace that had given her a second chance. She carved her future out of her past.

That's what David tells Israel to do. "Remember the grace of your God," he says. "Remember the kindness, the forgiveness, the tenderness and care. Remember God's grace—and transform that memory into your future."

∾

Our eyes, Lord, are focused on scenes that rush past us in the present: today's newspaper, today's television programs, today's computer printout. Gather us aside in the quiet of our memories, and remind us of the grace that brought us this far. Excite us once more with memories of your care, love, forgiveness, and encouragement. In Christ, Amen.

Memories That Kill, Memories That Heal

Read Philippians 1:3-11

I thank my God every time I remember you.
—Philippians 1:3

We have so many memories, don't we? Memories of successes and failures. Memories of what others have done to us, and we to them. Who of us can call up memories without appreciating the power of grace and forgiveness?

Have you ever talked to someone whose marriage was falling apart? He remembers so much: the bitter words, the angry arguments, the nasty phone calls.

At first you sympathize. But after a while, you notice that the stories always conclude a certain way, that every tale ends with blame, that his memory is selective. You begin to realize that he's building a defense for what he plans to do. He's laying the groundwork, right or wrong, for the divorce. His past shapes his future.

We all use our past to mold our future—we build our future on memories of the past. The challenge is to determine what memories we will select to shape our future. As you well know, not all marriages fail. Some couples are always celebrating anniversaries and retelling stories of how they found each other, loved each other, supported each other. These couples are shaping their future, too. They are building their lives through memories that confirm their relationship.

Sometimes that's what we have to do with our faith. We have to take the best of our past and relive it. We have to replay the past and use it to chart our course for the future.

Not long ago I spent an evening with a middle-aged couple who had disappeared from church life. They had lost their faith, they told me.

How did it happen? Was there a crisis in their life? Did God let them down? Were they taken by another religion?

No, they said, their faith had just slipped away over time. First they were caught up in their business. Then they traveled a lot. Then they were busy with other things. Along the way, they stopped going to church. Gradually they stopped believing in God.

After listening for a while, I gently led them to their room called Remember. I asked them about God and about their parents' beliefs. I asked them about the songs they learned years ago when they were growing up in Holland.

They laughed a little at first, remembering things they hadn't thought about in a long time. A gleam came to their eyes as one memory jogged another, and the stories tumbled out. At last the tears began to flow.

These people hadn't lost their faith. They had just forgotten it. They had neglected their room called Remember too long. When they finally went back, when they opened that door once again, when they stumbled across that threshold anew and felt the comfort of the room, they found their faith in God waiting for them.

~

Who am I, Lord? In the rush of life I've pressed ahead, but I'm not sure I've always known what I was doing. Take me back in time today. Bring the scenes of my life into focus. Take me back to the room called Remember, and let me find my faith. Amen.

Our Greatest Treasure

Read 1 Corinthians 11:23-26

"Do this in remembrance of me."
—1 Corinthians 11:24

It was the last night Jesus and his disciples would spend together. The next day Jesus would go the way of the cross.

He told them of his departure. You'll see me for a little while longer, he said, but then I'm going away. He told them of the grief that would fill their hearts.

Then he told them something more difficult. Eventually you will all forget me, he said. They couldn't believe it. They couldn't believe their memories would be so poor or their faith so shallow.

But Jesus didn't scold them. Instead, he told them two more things. First, he said he would send the Holy Spirit to remind them of their time together. The Holy Spirit would jog their memories—help them remember who they were and who Jesus was.

Next, Jesus told them about the room called Remember. He told them to come together every now and then. Take some bread, he said, and break it. When you do, remember my broken body. Take a cup, he said, and pass it around. As you drink from it, remember the color of my blood, gushing as it will from the cross.

Then your faith will return, he said. You'll find it there, in the room called Remember.

Several years ago, Fred Ferre spoke to a group of theology students about the source of his father's faith. His father was Nels Ferre, a distinguished theologian and author.

Nels came from a family of ten in Sweden. At thirteen, he was sent to find his future in America on his own. At the train station on the day of his departure, Nels's family surrounded him, holding hands as his father led in prayer. Then each member of the family said a prayer. That was his last earthly contact with his family.

Nels boarded the train and sat by the window, watching his family wave to him and cry. As the train rolled out of the station, his mother ran down the wooden platform alongside it. He slid the window open and leaned out just in time to hear her calling, "Nels! Nels! Remember Jesus! Remember Jesus!"

That's what we're doing in these brief moments together. Remembering Jesus. Remembering God's love for us. Remembering what it means to be what we were meant to be.

There are many other things we could be doing right now, but is anything more important than stopping for a while in the room called Remember? Than carving our future out of our past? Than experiencing our faith again?

"A man's real possession," said Alexander Smith, "is his memory." He was right. How rich are you today? Why don't you go back to the room called Remember and find out?

~

Search me, O God, and know my heart. Test my anxious thoughts. See what ways of the Spirit reside within me, and lead me in the way everlasting! Amen.

Week 3
When God
Lets Us Down

Nazi death camp survivor Elie Wiesel wrote a book
called *The Trial of God*, which retells the story of great
atrocities committed in the town of Shamgorod in 1649.
As beautiful Hanna, daughter of Jewish innkeeper
Berish, is preparing for her wedding, the Christian citizens of Shamgorod explode with angry violence, killing
all the Jews in their town except Berish and Hanna,
whom they horribly mistreat.

When a roving band of Jewish musicians arrives to
celebrate the Feast of Purim, there's little cause for fes-
tivity. But since the feast must be observed, Berish sug-
gests that they hold a trial to accuse God of all his crimes
against the human race.

Berish says, "I want to understand why he is giving
strength to the killers and nothing but tears and the
shame of helplessness to the victims."

We all struggle with similar thoughts, don't we? Even
if we haven't been hurt in life as badly as Elie Wiesel or
Berish the innkeeper, we've all been troubled more than
once by the problem of God's silence when our pain
mounts up.

Betrayed!

Read Psalm 55

If an enemy were insulting me, I could endure it. . . .
But it is you, . . . my close friend.
—Psalm 55:12, 13

Charles Wolfe tells of a summer he spent as counselor at a boys' camp in Texas. One day he saw two young fellows hunched over, watching a scorpion skit along in the dust.

"I was stung by a scorpion once," declared one boy proudly. "What did it feel like?" asked the other. The fellow pinched his arm until the pain reached a certain level. Then he reached over and pinched his friend's arm. "Hmm," said the friend. "I thought it would hurt more than that."

Pain is relative, isn't it? What hurts me may not hurt you. On the other hand, what brings tears to your eyes may have little effect on me. The only thing that's certain is that we all experience pain and suffering. One Spanish philosopher put it this way: "What is this life that begins amidst the cries of the infant and the screams of the mother?" We come into the world wailing and often leave it that way, too. To live is to know suffering firsthand.

Some kinds of pain are worse than others, of course. A cut finger, a bruised knee—they hurt for a while but don't slow us down. Major surgery? That's higher on our list of hurts. Job loss? Financial worries? Relocation? Experts tell us these events produce more stress than most other traumas in life. Psychological pain cuts much deeper than physical pain. Alfred Hitchcock and Stephen King have applied that knowledge successfully—they both know how to press the right panic buttons in our souls.

What tops our list of hurts? Death, perhaps—the death of a friend, a parent, a child, a spouse. Certainly few things in life cause more pain than death. Death is the sting of sin, the Bible says. You can imagine the old scorpion crawling up from hell to cast his tail about in fury and frustration, dragging us down in pain through the dust of death.

But is death the *worst* of all hurts? I know a man who puts something else at the top of his list: betrayal. Years ago, his business partner turned on him. This was a man he called friend, someone to whom he entrusted his livelihood, the one who shared his struggles. If I told you the details of the betrayal, you wouldn't believe it. No one could possibly be that mean, especially to a friend! And that's precisely why it hurts so much, even now, years later.

Or take the case of a woman I know. She almost wishes her husband had died. Then she would at least be left with good memories of their marriage. But instead, he ran off one day with another woman. How can she accept that? He was her best friend, her closest confidant, her intimate partner. And now he's with another woman, as if that's the way it was meant to be.

She doesn't want to keep thinking about it, but what can she do? The hurt is so deep, so painful, so caustic. If you ask her what tops her list of hurts, she'll tell you with tears in her eyes.

Our lists of hurts differ, but most of us would agree that nothing hurts more than betrayal. A friend who turns her back on you. A spouse who leaves. A community that disowns you. Across the pages of history, the moments of betrayal stand out—Brutus's betrayal of Caesar, Judas's betrayal of Jesus, Stalin's betrayal of his countrymen. The greatest pain in life is to feel the knife in the back and then to turn and see the face of one we trusted, one we leaned on, one we felt close to.

In Psalm 55, David cries with the pain of betrayal. Fortunately, his tears become a prayer. When others have let us down, we can pray with David, "As for me, I trust in you."

∾

There are times, God, when we don't know where to turn. We've been hurt too deeply for words, burned too badly to trust, betrayed by the very ones who promised to stand with us. Do you know what we feel? Let us sense that you still see us, still know us, still care about us. Amen.

Your Worst Nightmare

Read Psalm 88

I cry to you for help, O LORD. . . .
Why, O LORD, do you reject me?
—Psalm 88:13, 14

The pain of betrayal tops our list. But what if the one who betrayed us was God? What would we do then? How could we cope with that?

God betraying us? That's a tough concept, but it's what we seem to find in Psalm 88. Listen to these words: "You have put me in the lowest pit. . . . You have overwhelmed me with all your waves. You have taken from me my closest friends and have made me repulsive to them" (vv. 6-8). These are words of betrayal, spoken to God. I cry to you for help, says the psalmist, and you reject me.

What do we do when we feel the way the psalmist felt? Do you know what most people do? They stop going to church. They give up their faith. They forget about God. They say, "If he's going to treat me that way, he's out of my life!"

Probably no one has expressed these sentiments better than the novelist Peter De Vries. De Vries grew up in a Christian home but spent most of his life trying to sort out who God was to him. His most powerful novel, *The Blood of the Lamb*, is also his most tragic. It follows the career of Don Wanderhope.

Don's family believes in God. They trust that God holds all things in his hand, and they know he will always be there for them. Don, however, doesn't find this to be the case. One tragedy after another dogs him, and he wishes God wouldn't pay so much attention to him.

At the climax of the story, Don's wife bears them a daughter, the one spot of grace in her father's otherwise troubled existence. When his wife is diagnosed with leukemia, Don is even willing to give God another chance. He goes back to church and prays for her. He begs God to heal her, to touch her life with relief.

But she dies anyway. Don leaves the hospital carrying the birthday cake they were going to share together. He walks past a church. Hanging over the doorway is a life-size statue of Christ on the cross. Taking the cake in his hand, he throws it at Jesus. Icing drips from the face like blood.

That's Don's final prayer. That's what he thinks of the God who betrayed him.

Have you been there? Many of us have. I've heard one refrain again and again during my years as a pastor: "Why did God let this happen? How could God do this to us? Why doesn't God hear my prayers?"

As we ask these questions, we softly sing the slow dirge of Psalm 88. Times like these represent the lowest pit into which we can fall, the darkest night of the soul, the deepest depression. No one can order us back into the light at times like these. Worst of all are the trite platitudes we hear: "God must really know your great strength to give you a load like this to bear."

When I'm down there with Heman, moaning Psalm 88 through tormented lips, don't take cheap shots with your religious piety. I won't have it. You'll only drive me as far away from you as I feel from God.

❧

Sometimes it seems that you are not there, God. Or even if you are, you are silent and reproachful. What do we do then?

How Large Is My World?

Read Esther 3:12–4:16

Urge her to go into the king's presence to beg for mercy and
plead with him for her people.
—Esther 4:8

When God lets us down, there are no easy answers, and I'm not going to propose any. But I do want to share four questions we should ask ourselves during times when Psalm 88 seems to be the only song we can sing.

The first question is this: How large is my world?

This question is important because we live in an age that has taught us the value of the individual—I'm important; I count; I have rights. It's good to live at a time when companies stress customer service, when computers are user friendly, when children are protected, and when slavery is gone. It's good to live in an age that emphasizes human dignity.

But there's a danger involved in focusing too much on the value of the individual. A society that stresses the individual runs the risk of placing our egos at the center of the universe.

In an earlier generation, people polished mirrors round and round until tiny scratches spread across the surface. When a candle was placed in front of a mirror, light was reflected round and round, in thousands of circles, with the flame at the center. So it is in our society. My life is at the center. My needs are the greatest. My concerns must be met first. Society owes me. Life owes me. God owes me. God becomes my servant, and I send him on errands. If God doesn't do what I ask, I pout, and I get angry, and I feel betrayed.

A minister once spoke at a convention in a great city. The convention hall was located in the heart of the slums. Wealthy Christians from all over the region gathered at the convention, securing their cars behind fenced enclosures and scurrying along under the streetlights to reach the safety of the building.

After the meeting, a woman spoke to the minister. She had everything money could buy, but she complained that God had let her down, that God didn't answer her prayers.

The minister felt sick. Yes, every heart knows suffering, every life is touched by grief, every family bears secret burdens. But, people, he thought, how big is your world? God let you down? What about those who live on these streets? What about those who don't even have the resources to wonder whether God let them down? How big is your world?

A Sunday school teacher, after teaching the story of the Good Samaritan, asked her class, "Now, what does this parable teach you?"

A little boy answered, "It means that if I get into trouble, my neighbors should help me."

Do you see what he did? He flipped the story around. If I'm in trouble, others had better help me. Or, in another context, if I'm in trouble, God had better help me. The spirit of our age says God owes me one—and when God doesn't perform on cue, he lets me down.

Maybe your hurts are unbearable today. Maybe the pain is raw and sharp. Maybe the agony of your soul shuts down your world so all you can see is the throbbing of your heavy heart.

But remember the prayer in the garden of one who also agonized in unbearable pain. Remember that he prayed for himself three times, "Father, take this bitter cup away from me!" And remember that the Father said no.

Did the Father let Jesus down? Did the Father betray him? No. For they both knew that the world was larger than the one man who prayed for relief. And because of that larger world, God delayed the relief he might have otherwise brought.

How large is your world? You need to ask that question, don't you? You need to ask it before you are swallowed up in self-pity.

~

There are hurts in my life that drag me down, Lord.
Sometimes it seems I'm all alone in my struggles. But when
I get to the point of self-pity, open my eyes to the needs of
others. I don't ask to be a martyr; I only ask to have the
compassion of Christ. In him, Amen.

How Rich Is My Spirit?

Read 2 Corinthians 1:3-11

*[God] comforts us in all our troubles, so that we can
comfort those in any trouble.*
—*2 Corinthians 1:4*

Here's another question we should ask ourselves when God seems to
have let us down: How rich is my spirit?

We know that Christianity is a religion of comfort. Paul says it so
clearly in the opening paragraphs of his second letter to the Corinthian
church. If our religion didn't bring us comfort, it would be a sorry religion
indeed.

But Christianity is not a *comfortable* religion. The comfort of our faith
doesn't mean a life of pleasantness, carefree bliss, and freedom from pain.
When I experience pain, God hasn't left me or betrayed me. After all,
what does the cross of Christ signify? And what did Jesus mean when he
said, "If anyone would come after me, he must deny himself and take up
his cross and follow me" (Matt. 16:24)?

Listen to these beautiful lines by the nineteenth-century American
poet John Greenleaf Whittier:

> Drop thy still dews of quietness,
> Till all our strivings cease;
> Take from our souls the strain and stress,
> And let our ordered lives confess
> The beauty of thy peace.

That's a wonderful prayer, and blessed is the person who experiences
that kind of peace. Whittier must have known it, at least when he penned
that verse.

But what did peace mean for Whittier? When some read his poetry,
they see him as a Christian mystic, cloistered in a quiet room, light flow-
ing in the windows, music and art surrounding him. There, they say, he
must have written his gentle poems, his pious prayers, his consoling verse.

But that's not an accurate picture. Whittier was a social reformer who
spent a lifetime promoting freedom for slaves and dignity for all people.
He was a traveling speaker. Picture him arriving at a hall in Concord,

New Hampshire, facing the crowd with his convictions—convictions formed in Scripture, at the knee of Jesus. Picture him being pelted with rotten eggs until his black Quaker coat runs yellow with stains. Picture him lampooned in the press, derided as a traitor.

When he was old and had published much, Whittier wrote, "I set a higher value on my name as appended to the Anti-Slavery Declaration of 1833 than on the title-page of any book."

How did he get a soul that deep? How did he gain such richness of spirit? It came from years of tortured faithfulness to God. Even when it seemed that God had let him down, he carried on, because he wasn't looking for a religion of ease; he was looking for a religion of righteousness and truth.

Has your God let you down? Has God failed you and ignored your cries? Ask yourself this question: How deep is my spirit? And when you plumb the depths of your soul, you will find that God has given you the profound capacity to know pain, to feel suffering, and to agonize over loss.

The world has betrayed us into shallow thinking, shallow feeling, shallow living. Deep living brings with it deep hurts. Deep souls know deep pain. But deep hearts also flow rich with love and patience, care and concern.

There's no excuse for pain in this world. God never said there was. Nor did he promise to remove it from your life. God only promised to bring an end to sin and evil and despair. And if your spirit is deep enough to know that, you will understand that God hasn't let you down.

Knowing that God has not let us down doesn't take the pain away, but it keeps it under control. In hope. In anticipation. That's the comfort of our religion, isn't it?

∼

Test the depths of my spirit, God, and help me know just how rich I am in love and compassion and care. Lead me to peace through mission and to comfort through the march of righteousness. I pray this in the name of Jesus, who showed me the path to follow. Amen.

How Long Is My View?

Read Hebrews 11:1-10; 12:1-3

He was looking forward.
—Hebrews 11:10

Here's the third question we should ask during those troublesome times when it seems as though God has forsaken us: How long is my view?

Pain is usually sharpest the instant it is inflicted. I can no longer call to mind the intensity of the pain I felt when I had a bicycle accident as a teenager. The Bible says that after a woman has given birth, she no longer remembers the excesses of her labor pains. It's the same with betrayal. The only way we can keep the pain alive is by replaying over and over in our minds the moment the agony was inflicted.

Every book by Jewish Nobel Peace Prize winner Elie Wiesel relives the horror of the Holocaust. Wiesel intends his writings to hurt, because he wants to keep the pain alive. He wants to remind people of the ungodly betrayal of Hitler, the unthinkable betrayal of the Nazis, and the incredible betrayal of German Christians. They turned their backs on their fellow human beings. They called on God to bless them and sent God's people to the gas chambers.

Although remembering our painful experiences can be constructive, it can also be destructive. Isn't life in the present challenging enough without dwelling on past hurts? Don't we already know in our hearts how great our agony is? Why cling to it, then, and replay it without end?

Sometimes the healing of our hurts starts only when we find another song to sing. Take the story of Helen, for instance. She had her sights set on a law degree from Ohio Wesleyan College. But then the flu epidemic of 1918 hit, taking her father as a victim. Suddenly everything had changed. Helen couldn't go to college; she had to get a job to support her mother.

The next ten years, Helen worked for an electrical utility. Just when she thought she was destined to remain lonely and unmarried, young Franklin Rice stepped in. He was a dashing entrepreneur, an up-and-coming banker. When they married in 1928, Helen's future was bright with promise.

A year later, the stock market crashed, and Franklin's financial world fell apart. He couldn't take the pressure, so he committed suicide.

Read the litany of Helen's life: a deceased father, a lost career, a vanished fortune, a dead husband, a lonely existence. Where is God when it hurts?

You may know Helen better than you realize. You see, she eventually took a job with the Gibson Greeting Card company. Helen Steiner Rice became a folk poet who spoke the language of thousands of Christians.

Some years ago Helen was asked which poem she thought was her best. She couldn't tell, she said, but she did know which one meant the most to her. It was this:

> So together we stand at life's crossroads
> And view what we think is the end.
> But God has a much bigger vision
> And he tells us it's only a bend.
> For the road goes on and is smoother,
> And the pause in the song is a rest.
> And the part that's unsung and unfinished
> Is the sweetest and richest and best.
> So rest and relax and grow stronger.
> Let go and let God share your load.
> Your work is not finished or ended;
> You've just come to a bend in the road.

Are you in pain today? Do you feel as if God has betrayed you? Then pause for a moment and ask yourself, How long is my view?

Your soul needs to know.

∼

When the road seems too long, Lord, when the path looks too rough; when my burdens are heavy and my sighs have gone gruff, pick me up for a moment; let me stand near your face. Show me where your strength leads me as I wander this maze. Point beyond the next turn, Lord, and give me a map. Let the light of the future beckon toward the next lap. And when courage falters, when heartache sets in, carry me through the dark midnight hours; let me rise with your dawn once again. Amen.

How True Is My God?

Read Isaiah 46

"To whom will you compare me?"
—Isaiah 46:5

How large is my world? How rich is my spirit? How long is my view? We need to ask these questions in the dark times of our lives. Here's a fourth one: How true is my God?

What I mean by the fourth question is this: is the picture of God that I have in my mind an accurate picture of the God of the Bible? When I say, "God has betrayed me," do I really know the God I'm talking about?

If I told you today that my wife has betrayed me, you would feel terrible with me, right? But then if I told you that she betrayed me by not writing this meditation for me, you wouldn't feel so bad anymore, would you? If I thought my wife should do my work for me, I would have a false concept of who she is.

Sometimes we make similar mistakes in our faith. Perhaps we have a certain picture of God: who God is, how God acts, and what God should do for us. But maybe that picture isn't true to who God is.

One man may say that God is cruel and heartless, always demanding, always forcing us to do things we don't want to do, always peering over our shoulders lest we step out of line. Maybe this man says he's lost his faith, that he doesn't believe in God anymore, that God let him down. Probably so. But where did he find that God in the first place? Certainly not in the Bible!

Or a woman may say that God doesn't answer her prayers. She used to be a believer, but when God didn't heal her husband's cancer, she decided to stop worshiping him. God let her down. Maybe so. But is God Santa Claus? Certainly not the God of the Bible!

I remember flying to Edmonton once for a meeting. I had been told that someone would meet me at the airport, but I waited at the terminal for several minutes and no one came for me. I saw one man watching me, but when I walked over to him, he turned away. So I took a taxi.

When I got to the meeting, there he was—the man I had seen in the airport! After everyone had been introduced, he came over to me and apologized profusely. "I came to pick you up," he said, "and I saw you there. But I had a picture of you in my mind, and you didn't look at all like it. So I said to myself, 'No, that can't be him!'"

This story illustrates why we sometimes think God has let us down—perhaps our picture of God is not true to life. If we buy a shirt with a collar that's too tight, we won't wear it. If we have a belt that's two inches too short, we'll never put it on. And in our faith life, if our picture of God is different from the true God, God will always let us down. Our God and our faith won't match. So we will leave God hanging in the closet or throw him out with the garbage.

Then we'll say we tried religion once, but it let us down. But the real problem is that we haven't found the true God!

⁓

Lord, teach us who you are. Shake our feeble notions of who you are and help us find the broader reaches of your personality and power. Let your Word be our guide and your Spirit our instructor. And let us never cease to look at your human face in our Lord Jesus. Amen.

Beyond Betrayal

Read 2 Corinthians 4

We are hard pressed on every side, but not crushed; perplexed,
but not in despair; persecuted, but not abandoned; struck
down, but not destroyed.
—*2 Corinthians 4:8-9*

No pain is greater than the pain of betrayal. And no night of the soul is darker than that in which God seems the oppressor—the fiend rather than the friend.

I've known dark nights in my own life, and I've spent many pastoral hours in hospital wards and lonely apartments. But I've learned that in days of great hurting I need to ask myself these four questions: How large is my world? How rich is my spirit? How long is my view? and How true is my God? These questions do not solve all the riddles of my faith, but they help me keep the realities of my faith in focus.

Think of Horatio Spafford, a lawyer in Chicago in the latter half of the nineteenth century. When Mrs. O'Leary's cow overturned the lantern the night of October 8, 1871, the great fire that resulted destroyed Spafford's home and business. Worse yet, the Spaffords' only son, a six-year-old, was killed.

These disasters put a heavy strain on the family. Mrs. Spafford became so nervous and run-down that her doctor recommended a vacation, so the family laid plans to sail for Europe in November of 1873.

As the date approached, Horatio realized he was too busy to leave with his family. He sent his wife and four daughters on ahead, planning to catch up with them later.

On November 22, the ship carrying the five Spafford women sank beneath the waves of the north Atlantic. Nearly everyone on board died. On December 1, Mrs. Spafford sent a telegram to Horatio from Cardiff, Wales. It said, "Saved alone!"

How much more would one couple have to suffer? Where was God in all of this?

Horatio left immediately to join his wife. As he crossed the Atlantic, he asked the captain to show him where the other ship had gone down. When they came to the spot, Horatio stood at the rail, looking out at the cruel gray sea. Did he cry out to God in pain? Probably so. Did he feel cheated by life? Undoubtedly. Did he turn away from God, saying God had let him down?

He could have. But he didn't, because in those moments he wrote these words:

> When peace like a river attendeth my way,
>   when sorrows like sea billows roll;
> whatever my lot, thou hast taught me to say,
>   "It is well, it is well with my soul."
>
> Though Satan should buffet, though trials should come,
>   let this blest assurance control:
> that Christ has regarded my helpless estate,
>   and has shed his own blood for my soul.
>
> O Lord, haste the day when my faith shall be sight,
>   the clouds be rolled back as a scroll;
> the trump shall resound and the Lord shall descend;
>   even so, it is well with my soul.

In the trials of our lives, Lord, give us the grace to find faith
that looks beyond the moment to the hope that never dims.
Let the trials of Christ strengthen our courage as we
follow in his footsteps. Amen.

Week 4
A Life of
Quotation Marks

Punctuation marks are strange things. They're not words, yet without them, words often make no sense. We don't pronounce them, yet we know immediately when they're missing.

Quotation marks are my favorite type of punctuation. They may be a nuisance to type or write, but they reflect, in some measure, the importance of relationships and communication in society. They also acknowledge the depth of our debt to others for what we have learned from them. Without quotation marks—which credit others for insights they have given us—we live mighty shallow lives.

MEDITATION 22

Plagiarism

Read Ecclesiastes 1:1–10

There is nothing new under the sun.
—Ecclesiastes 1:9

One of the most traumatic incidents in my life happened some years ago when I was teaching at the Reformed Theological College of Nigeria. As was the practice, I assigned the students in my fourth-year Old Testament Prophets class the task of writing an exegesis paper.

An exegesis is an in-depth analysis of a particular passage of Scripture. It examines themes and literary structure, meanings of words, historical context, theological implications, and so forth. In class, we discussed how to write the paper: what resources to use in the library, how to put it together, what conclusions to draw.

Every day I stopped by the library and saw my students hard at work. They looked up from their books and grinned broadly. They told me their papers were going to be so good and I would be so proud of them.

When the day of reckoning came, my students gleamed with pride. My hopes and expectations ran high. After class, I went straight home and sat down to read.

Immediately my heart sank. These weren't exegesis papers. These were pages and pages of quotations lifted directly from commentaries—without footnotes or credits. In some cases, the only original word in the paper was the student's name at the top of the first page. I could even detect style changes when a student had switched from copying out of one book to copying out of another.

English was a second language for my students, and they used it quite well. But technical jargon was far beyond them. Yet, technical terms were littered throughout their papers as if they were as common as the greetings we spoke each morning. The students pretended these words and ideas were their own, cheapening the authors' ideas by imitating them.

I went to the principal of the school and unburdened myself. He explained that plagiarism was a perpetual problem; every year he warned students against it, but it never stopped. "Do what you think is best," he advised me.

This is what I did. I took the students' papers to the library. For two days I searched through commentaries, word studies, and other theological resources, finding as many of the passages the students had copied as I could. I wrote the references on their papers. Then I gave an F to all twelve students.

Few experiences have torn me apart as much as this. My decision caused an awful stir at the school. Students from that class came to my door at all hours of the day to protest. "Sir," they said, "you told us to use the commentaries. You told us to read the books. You told us to find out what others were saying."

That's the problem, isn't it? You see, there's hardly an original thought in this world. The writer of Ecclesiastes said it years ago: "There is nothing new under the sun." Whatever is, has been before. So my students were caught in a predicament: I wanted them to use the wisdom and knowledge of others; yet at the same time I wanted them to speak their own thoughts, write their own words, and express their own ideas. After all, that's the only way to truly learn. A photocopier knows nothing. It may process thousands of pictures and billions of words, but it doesn't have intelligence of its own.

Some people are plagiarists of words and ideas. Others are plagiarists of faith. They go through the motions they have observed in other Christians. They say what others say and act as others do, but in the end they ring hollow. They demonstrate nothing of an authentic relationship with God.

Do you know anyone like that?

~

Sometimes I dare not look inside myself, Lord, for fear I'll find very little. Is my identity my own, or have I spent so much time copying others that I no longer know who I am? Do I have a faith that arises from my relationship with you, or am I merely going with the flow, following the desires of my parents, the pressures of my friends, or the pull of the church? Help me to learn from others of great faith without stooping to cheap imitation. In Christ, Amen.

Enriched by Others

Read 2 Timothy 4:1-13

Bring . . . my scrolls, especially the parchments.
—2 Timothy 4:13

A woman once told me of an interesting experience she had one Sunday. At church that morning, she said, her minister preached a sermon based on a text from one of the gospels. In the afternoon she went to a friend's church and heard a different minister preach a sermon from a text in the book of Acts.

But the two sermons, she said, were identical. They had the same structure, the same points, the same terminology, and the same conclusion! You may know how this happened—one or both of the ministers was using a sermon prepared by someone else, without making it his own through creative interaction with the text and ideas.

It was probably a good sermon; but under the circumstances, the message was cheapened, wasn't it? The message wasn't really taken from the Bible texts, for how can one sermon flow from two different passages of Scripture? Nor did it spring from the spiritual struggles of at least one of the ministers, for how can two men, with different personalities and different ministries, preach exactly the same sermon? It can't be done!

Plagiarism isn't right, even when ministers do it—maybe especially then. But there's another side to the coin. Poor is the person who plagiarizes, yet poorer still is the person who has no quotation marks in his life at all. The person who never reads a poem, learns a lesson, memorizes a song, or digs into a book. The person who thinks she can make it through life on her own resources, shaped by her own knowledge. Poor is the person who carries through life few quotation marks from the vast wealth and resources of others.

I have always been intrigued by Paul's final comments in his second letter to young Timothy. The letter was written from his final prison cell, and it may be the last thing he wrote before he died. In it, Paul hands Timothy a treasure of fatherly wisdom about pastoring the congregation at Ephesus. He ends by urging Timothy to come visit him and adds, "Bring my scrolls, especially the parchments."

Why were the parchments so important?

While we may never be sure of the answer, the request is weighted with meaning. Paul knew that learning was life. He knew that when he stopped reading, he stopped growing. He knew that through education we become richer, deeper, wiser people.

If you were locked up in prison with him, what would you need to survive? Food? Water? An hour of sunlight each day?

What about books? Are there quotation marks in your life—marks that show how broad and deep and wise your heart is becoming?

~

Lord, much of what I am today I have learned from others. Let me never stop learning and growing and expanding the horizons of my heart and mind. In Christ, Amen.

The Hidden Seas Within

Read Proverbs 22:17-21

Apply your heart to what I teach.
—*Proverbs 22:17*

Benjamin Weir, a Presbyterian minister, was a hostage in Lebanon for over a year, much of the time in solitary confinement. How did he survive? How did he keep his wits about him? By calling to mind Scripture passages and reciting verses he had memorized in his younger years. He says he stayed alive only by calling up the quotation marks in his memory.

I know two doctors at a hospital in London, Ontario—men with extremely busy schedules—who meet once a month over coffee to recite a sonnet they have memorized. Poetry is their gift to each other, a treasure they store in their minds—fourteen lines a month, twelve times a year.

These people know their inner resources, and they know they are nourished by the quotation marks they add to their lives.

Someone once said that the first half of our lives belongs to the extrovert—the person within us who is willing to get out and do things, to make waves, to achieve success in life. But the second half belongs to the introvert—the part of us that sits and thinks and remembers and feeds on the inner resources of our hearts and minds.

If this is true, what would happen if we reached the second half of life and found nothing inside? Listen to the words of Robert Louis Stevenson: "Here's a man who is forty years old, and he hasn't got two thoughts, the one to rub against the other, while he is waiting for the train."

Is Stevenson talking about someone you know? Do you have a treasure of quotation marks in your heart? Have you read the Bible through? Have you memorized the Psalms? Have you read the great classics of literature? Do you know the beauty of poetry?

The novelist Mary Prescott Montague was blind. One day she realized that her hearing was deteriorating; soon her world would be very small. "How will you cope?" someone asked her. Listen to her answer: "If the world be closed without, I'll sail the hidden seas within."

If your eyes were dimmed and your ears stopped, if your senses no longer brought you news of the world around, how far could you sail on the hidden seas within? Some people's hidden seas are like muddy swamps, shallow and stagnant. But others' are like broad and beautiful oceans. When they leave one port, they have resources to explore new continents and new horizons.

Years ago someone asked Edgar Frank where he came from. "Goshen," he said. "Goshen?" the questioner replied. "How can you live in a place like Goshen, where all people do is grow cabbages and spend their time talking to one another across the fences? How can you live there?"

Edgar Frank wrote a poem in reply. Oh, he said, "I don't live in Goshen! I may keep a house there. But others have given to me an enchantment that is broader than time or space! I live in Greece with Plato and Epictetus! I live in Rome where Cicero and Dante wrote, and where Michelangelo painted! And so I live in Paradise, not in Goshen!"

Do you know what Frank was talking about? Are you still going to school—the school of great literature, the school of great music, the school of the Bible? Is yours a life filled with quotation marks?

~

God of great wisdom, teach my heart through books and other treasures of learning in this fascinating world. Let me be tempted to study and dig into the wonderful things in life. Broaden the seas of my mind so I can sail them with delight, even in circumstances that would otherwise tear me down. I ask this in the name of the true Word of God, our Lord Jesus. Amen.

Heroes

Read Hebrews 11:17–12:1

We are surrounded by such a great cloud of witnesses.
—Hebrews 12:1

Abraham Kuyper is one of my heroes. Early this century, when he served as prime minister of the Netherlands, he brought Christianity into the political realm in a powerful way.

Faith wasn't always so important to Kuyper. At the start of his career, he was a young preacher in a rural village. He had been schooled in the best of modern theology, and his sermons were well-polished master-pieces.

Not all in his congregation were impressed, though. Pietronella Baltus didn't care for his preaching, and she spoke her mind to him more than once. Certainly his sermons were intelligent and well delivered, she said, but they did not declare the gospel of Jesus Christ.

Kuyper was intrigued. Who was this woman to serve as his critic? He began to visit her, and, over tea, she explained Jesus to him. She told him about faith and God and things outside of his experience. With her simple wisdom and vision, Pietronella Baltus silenced the knowledge of the great preacher. He knew his theology, but he didn't know her God. He knew his dogmatics, but he didn't know her Christ. He knew his church history, but he didn't know her Lord.

After sitting at her feet, Kuyper rose up a different man. For the rest of his life, he spoke of the woman who had changed his heart, opened his eyes, and swept the cobwebs out of his soul. She was his teacher, his friend, his miracle of faith. She lived on in his heart and mind, ever bracketed by quotation marks.

You see, the quotation marks of our lives surround not only the great ideas we've learned, but also the great people we've known. Autobiographies of great people always contain pages of thanks to those who taught and influenced the authors throughout their pilgrimage.

Harry Emerson Fosdick once contrasted the authority of a dictionary with the authority of a mother. A dictionary speaks with power, he said, but it always stays outside of us. A mother's authority, on the other hand, is entirely different. It is living and vital; it grabs us and sustains us from the inside.

According to Fosdick, "A man who has had the experience of great motherhood comes to feel that if his mother thinks something very strongly and very persistently, he would better consider that thing well, for the chances are overwhelming that there is truth in it." The influence of life's heroes doesn't let go of us easily. Our heroes are stamped between the quotation marks of our hearts.

If you were to rewrite Hebrews 11 based on your own experience, what names would you put there? What faces and personalities pop up in your mind? How rich is your heritage of heroes who sustained you along the way? Which mentors, teachers, and friends are bracketed between the quotation marks of your soul?

~

Give me time, today, Lord, to remember the names and faces of those who have filled my life with meaning. Show me again the people who have brought out the best in me, who have shaped the contours of my soul, and who have molded the values of my heart. Teach me to recite my list of "heroes of faith" with joy and appreciation. Amen.

Seeing the Unseen

Read Psalm 16

I have set the LORD always before me.
—Psalm 16:8

Many centuries ago, the great theologian Cyprian said that a person who has God as his father, has the church as his mother. Why? Because the church is the means by which God strengthens and deepens and restores our faith. We learn of God from the psalms, hymns, and spiritual songs of the church. We see God in the testimonies of the saints. When we've lost our way, the church whispers to us of the one who lives within her and draws us back to him.

Recently *Canadian Living* magazine published an article entitled "The Comforting Pew." Young families are feeding their spiritual hunger by going back to church, the story said. Featured in the article was a freelance editor from Toronto who had returned to church after many years because she knew God was around but couldn't find him on her own.

Syndicated columnist Robert Fulghum tells the same story in another way. Long ago, he says, he gave up any significant relationship with God. He didn't really want God, the church, or religion to cramp his style.

Then he met someone who prevented him from banishing God from his life. He was so amazed that he put her picture on the mirror above the sink where he washes each morning. Every time he cleans his hands, she's there to cleanse his heart. Whenever he scrubs his face, she's there to wash his soul.

He met her a few years ago in Oslo, Norway, during the Nobel prize ceremonies. He was standing among the crowd of guests that filled the doors and hallways of the auditorium.

Then she passed by. She stopped for a moment and smiled at him. For a brief moment, it seemed as if she reached into his heart and understood him. There was no condemnation in her look, only genuine care. Then she went to the front of the auditorium to receive the Nobel Peace Prize from the hand of the king of Norway. It was Mother Teresa of Calcutta.

Somehow, said Fulghum, she reminded me of the things that were missing in my life—the quotation marks that hung empty, the meaning that had slipped away.

A couple of years later, he met her again, this time in Bombay. She was speaking at an international conference in a large hotel. There she stood, in her sandals and sari, a simple person in a very complex world.

"We can do no great things," she said, "only small things with great love." With that, says Fulghum, "she upsets me, disturbs me, shames me. What does she have that I do not?"

But he knows. Deep inside, he knows. That's why he keeps her picture on his mirror. That's why he looks into her eyes again and again. That's why he writes about her. He knows that between the quotation marks of her life, she has God. That's the source of her strength, her energy, her inner beauty.

He that has God as his Father, said Cyprian, has the church as his mother. And, in the church, as Mother Teresa would be the first to testify, you find the great Quotation that makes your life matter. In the church you find the Word. The Word of God incarnate. The Word that feeds all the other quotations of life.

❧

Word of God, teach me to know what others have discovered, that life begins with you. Lead me back to the church, and make my life richer by broadening the quotations of my heart with yourself. Lord, speak to me that I may speak in living echoes of your voice. Amen.

The Urge to Share

Read Luke 19:28-40

"If they keep quiet, the stones will cry out."
—Luke 19:40

In his *Reflections on the Psalms*, C. S. Lewis asks himself an interesting question: What would be the worst thing that could happen to me? His answer is intriguing. He says the very worst thing that could happen would be to have something wonderful occur in his life and have no one to share it with. You read a good book, he says, and you can't tell anyone about it. You see a lovely sunset, but you're all alone, so you say it out loud: Oh, God! What a beautiful sunset! You know a good story, but there's no one who would understand it. These are the worst things that could happen to me, says Lewis.

He's right, in a way. Can you imagine loving a person deeply and not being able to speak of your love? It's the stuff of heartbreaking novels. It's the kind of thing that makes us ache. Gordon Lightfoot sings in hopeful sadness, "If you could read my mind, Love, what a tale my thoughts would tell."

When we feel something deeply, we have to tell others about it. This is especially true with the treasures held between the quotation marks of our lives.

Listen to this story from the life of Jascha Heifetz, a world-renowned violinist. Once Heifetz hired a new secretary and told the young man, "You don't need to compliment me after every performance. If I play well, I know it myself. And if I don't, I shall only think less of you if you try to flatter me."

So the secretary did his best to please the master. Never, after a performance, did he mention a word about Heifetz's talent.

One night Heifetz outdid himself with brilliance. The concert was spectacular. The glory of the music demanded a response of praise, but the dutiful secretary kept his mouth shut. Heifetz became more and more agitated with the young man until he finally shouted, "What's the matter with you? Don't you like music?"

We all need to share the things that move us deeply. We need to offer to others the treasures we've collected between the quotation marks of our lives. Most of all, we have to share the depth of our relationship with God.

Do you remember the story of Helen Keller? She was blind and deaf from her earliest years. When she was a little girl and had just begun to speak with her hands, Phillips Brooks came to her to teach her something about God.

As he started to explain "God" to her, Helen got so excited. She had always known about God, she signed back, but until now she hadn't known God's name. How thankful she was to finally express praise to the God she had loved in her soul!

The function of a computer can be summarized by the phrase "Data in, data out." For humans, a similar phrase applies: "Treasures in, blessings out." To make life more complete, we simply have to share what is on our hearts. You can quote me on that!

~

Thank you, God, for the treasures you have given us through books and learning, music and artists, teachers and friends, parents and lovers. Thanks most of all for the riches of your Word and Spirit. And thank you for the urge to share the wealth of our hearts with others. Amen.

Doxology

Read 1 John 3:11–24

---

*Let us not love with words or tongue but
with actions and in truth.*
—1 John 3:18

When the theologian Geoffrey Wainwright wrote a summary of his theology a few years ago, he called the resulting work *Doxology*, a song of praise to God. But he found all his words inadequate to convey what his theology meant for living. So he pulled his doctrinal treatises together with this story.

Many years ago, Turkish soldiers raided an Armenian home. The officer in charge ordered the parents killed and gave the daughters to his soldiers to be raped and brought home as slaves. He kept the oldest daughter for himself, using her again and again in despicable ways.

One day, the oldest daughter escaped. After she found her life again, she trained to be a nurse. But when she was finally assigned to a hospital, she discovered that her ward was filled with Turkish officers.

Late one night, her old enemy was brought in. By the light of the lantern, she could see he was near death. She wouldn't have to try to kill him—with a little neglect, he'd be gone.

But the man didn't die. As the days passed, he recovered strength. One morning the doctor told him how fortunate he was. The doctor pointed to the young nurse and said, "But for her devotion to you, you would be dead."

Recognizing her, the officer asked, "Why didn't you kill me?" She simply replied, "I am a follower of him who said, 'Love your enemies.'"

That's quoting at its deepest, isn't it? It's a life that has learned love and then become love. It's a spirit that knows life and breathes life in response. It's a soul that has found peace with God and then creates peace in relationships with others.

If our faith is strong, it is only because we have found the living Word of God between the quotation marks of our lives. God has been speaking to us all along. Our Maker has become the great quotation of our lives, the Alpha and Omega, the beginning and end of all we see and know and feel and say.

The Russian writer Tolstoy said he truly lived only at those times when he believed in God. "To know God and to live are one and the same thing," he said. Deep down, we know how true that is. Paul put it this way: "For to me, to live is Christ" (Phil. 1:21).

Is your life filled with quotation marks? Can you sail the seas of your heart and find the riches of your spirit piled up high? Are you sharing the heritage of your quotations with those who will follow you? And between the first and last quotation marks in your life, do you find the face of God?

∽

Before my life began, Lord, you thought it into being. Throughout my life you have read into me the great quotations that have enriched my spirit. Let me live them now, in love and service. And let me find you always, when I look within. Amen.

Week 5
Reflections on Pierced Ears

It is incredible to me why people endure the pain of having their ears pierced just to wear a blob of gold on their ears. I remember tagging the ears of our animals when I was a boy on the farm. At least the pain we put the animals through had a constructive purpose!

Fashion has its own purpose, and it is not always efficiency or practicality. In fact, good fashion often emerges from lines that are presented in a new way, or from shapes and forms that jar the senses because they are unexpected and unusual.

On some level, art and fashion function symbolically. They remind us of qualities of life that have escaped us too long: beauty, joy, intimacy, grace. And if pierced ears play a role in that reminder, maybe they're worth the pain.

Fashion Statements

Read Psalm 40:1-8

My ears you have pierced.
—Psalm 40:6

Fashion in our culture seems to dictate the necessity of pierced ears. When my daughters were in elementary school, they reported at the start of each year which classmates had gotten their ears pierced over the summer. Then came the inevitable plea, "Please can I get my ears pierced too?"

This always made me smile, remembering the arguments that erupted when I was a youngster and my older sister talked about getting her ears pierced. The idea of pierced ears created a tremendous theological debate at our home. How dare she even think about it, my parents said; if God wanted people to have holes in their ears, he would have put them there in the first place!

The issue of pierced ears arose some years ago in a new context when a member of my congregation spoke with me about one of our Sunday school teachers. She expressed concern that this teacher was not suitable for the job.

My heart did a flip-flop. "Why not?" I asked. "What's the problem?" Had she found out an awful secret about this teacher? I didn't know of anything wrong.

Then it came out. The teacher had pierced ears. Actually, I should say, *he* had *one* pierced ear and wore a single earring. Can you imagine that? How times had changed.

I guess if anybody could imagine that, it would be David. Notice what he says to God in the sixth verse of Psalm 40? "Sacrifice and offering you did not desire, but my ears you have pierced."

That verse catches us off guard, doesn't it? What could David mean? Finding out takes a little digging, and we'll spend time exploring this mystery further in the coming week.

But let's get back to those fashion statements of today—those pierced ears that my sister wanted (and got), that my daughters wanted (and two of them got—the third decided against it after watching the pain her sisters went through), and that our Sunday school teacher sported (he later became one of the finest elders I've ever known).

If you read the rest of what David has to say in Psalm 40, you soon realize that physical appearances fade quickly when the character of the heart shines through. Maybe earrings are trendy fads; maybe they are truly fashion. But lives of devotion to God and care for others never go out of style.

~

When I dress each morning, Lord, give me the sense of beauty that comes from the graces of the heart. Let me wear with delight the fruit of the Spirit: love, joy, peace, patience, kindness, goodness, faithfulness, gentleness, and self-control. Let the words of my mouth and the meditations of my heart be pleasing in your sight, my Lord and my God! Through Christ, Amen.

Down and Out in Palestine

Read Exodus 19:1-6; 21:1-4

"If you buy a Hebrew servant..."
—Exodus 21:2

You know the story. The Israelites were slaves in Egypt. For forty years, God prepared Moses to be a leader. Then he matched him up in a duel with Pharaoh's magicians, creating a spectacular display of hideous natural disasters that will forever define the meaning of the word *plague*. God and Moses won, of course, and now the Israelites stand free at the foot of Mount Sinai. In the thunder and clouds above, God breathes a covenant, and the nation of Israel takes shape.

God's "laws" are all couched in scenes from everyday life. Suppose . . ., says God. Suppose one of your neighbors is deeply in debt. Times are tough for him. He borrowed some money from you a while ago—a lot of money, actually—and he has fallen behind on his payments. In fact, it looks like he'll never get his financial situation in order.

But Israel doesn't have any bankruptcy laws. Your neighbor can't just file a legal document, default on his debts, and start over again with a clean slate. It doesn't work that way.

This is what happens instead: He comes to you and he tells you he has no way to pay you. He has already sold his personal belongings. The little plot of land he inherited from his parents was snatched up long ago by other creditors.

What does he have left to offer you? Only himself. Only his strong back and aching muscles and the remaining years of his life. He becomes your slave, your indentured servant. He is your property now, and you put him to work in your fields. It's the only way you'll ever recover any of the huge debt he still owes you.

In most cultures of the ancient Near East, this would be the last word. The man would be your slave for the rest of his life. You could do with him whatever you wanted for as long as you wanted.

Not so in Israel. Our Lord doesn't delight in slavery and believes in giving people the chance to start over. So God builds safeguards into the system. Your neighbor can work as your slave for six years, but then he can go free. He needs the dignity of his freedom to survive, and the seventh year is his ticket back to independence. That's how God structured the system.

Amazing, isn't it? A system of justice built on grace! A society that takes responsibility seriously but balances it with compassion. It's the kind of society we all long for.

Second chances are important to us. Do you remember the story of Anastasia, the woman who claimed to be the long-lost daughter of the last emperor of Russia, Czar Nicholas II? She was found depressed and suicidal in an insane asylum. Through hypnosis, she recaptured a memory that seemed to confirm her place in royal history. Then the press got wind of the story and sensationalized it: Could this destitute woman be the heir to the Russian throne?

Only one person could prove it: Nicholas's mother. The old Empress, who was still alive in exile, was brought in. After a long visit with the young woman, she announced to the world, "Anna is my granddaughter!"

Anna never gained a place in royal society because the old woman's pronouncement only fueled the flames of controversy. But from that day on she began to live again. She blossomed as a person. Her suicide threats stopped. She washed her body with care and clothed it with dignity.

What caused her transformation? She explained by saying, "It never mattered whether or not I was a princess. It only matters that . . . someone, if it be only one, has held out their arms to welcome me back from death."

Sounds a lot like the gospel truth, doesn't it?

~

God of second chances, we thank you for the place in our lives
where justice and mercy embrace. May we never forget the
love that makes us live or the grace that turns us nobodies
into children of the King. And, in our dealings with
others, may we pass that redemption along.
Through Christ we pray, Amen.

A New Twist

Read Exodus 21:2-6

"He shall . . . pierce his ear with an awl."
—Exodus 21:6

Here comes a new twist on yesterday's story. Suppose, says God, that things have changed for your slave over the past few years. When he came to you, he was beaten apart by life. He had nowhere to run, nowhere to hide, no resources left.

Still, when he came to you that day, knowing he owed you his very body for the debt he couldn't repay, he resented being locked into slavery and bowing to you as his master.

But now, six years later, he sees things differently. For one thing, he has learned to respect you, even to like you. Secretly, he might go so far as to call you his friend. Yes, he's a slave, but you have treated him well. You've given him shelter and stability. He has begun to feel like part of your family, not just a piece of property.

Something else has happened, too. Some time ago you bought another slave—a young woman. Her father sold her to pay off some of his debts. Right from the start, the two got along well. In fact, you watched them fall in love. You noticed the way they treated each other, and you smiled at the tricks they pulled just to spend time together.

When they came to you to request permission to get married, you felt like a father to them. You gave your blessing and threw a big party for them.

But tomorrow the man's six years of slavery are over, and he's free to go. Technically his wife and children still belong to you, but for his sake, you're probably willing to free them with him. That's how close the two of you have become over the years.

Tonight he approaches you. He's serious. He has something on his heart, and you can see it will take him some time to get it out. He says, "When I came here six years ago, I was shattered. I couldn't even look you in the eye. I had let you down. Worse than that, I had let myself down. I couldn't pay my debts. I was a hopeless failure. My life was ruined.

"And you held my soul in your hands. There were times I wished you would crush me. There were days I felt as good as dead. But you were a fair man—firm, but fair. You made me work, but you gave me everything I needed.

"I have to tell you this: You're really like a father to me. In fact, I have a hard time thinking about leaving. All I am today I owe to you."

Then his eyes get misty. You can feel the tears pumping behind your cheeks, too. He chokes the sobs and goes on. "Would it be acceptable to you if I stayed here and continued as your servant? I have never been able to make it on my own. You've given me more dignity as your slave than I ever had when I was free."

Now the tears gush. You hug him as a son, and he kisses you as he would a father. Then, in the most touching ceremony of Israelite society, you pierce his earlobe and give him an earring to wear. He is now your servant for life—but no longer out of demand or debt or duty. Now he's your servant out of love.

Perhaps the most freeing thing we can experience is the bondage of love and commitment. Maybe that's why faith is more than a wish or a hope or a desire. Maybe the strength of faith is in the choices and commitments it makes.

We can go a step further. A faith that cannot make commitments may find itself drowning in a wash of swirling currents. Where is your faith today? You'll find it in the decisions and commitments you have made.

~

Lord our God, thank you for choosing us, for binding yourself to us in cords of love that cannot be broken. Help us to find our faith in the commitments we make to you and to the people around us. Amen.

Faith Is Public

Read Romans 1:8-17; 10:9-11

It is with your mouth that you confess.
—Romans 10:10

Faith that would be strong must be a public faith. That's why the Christian Reformed Church has a ceremony called Public Profession of Faith.

We all have private beliefs. We all have times of personal communion with God. We all like to sit and reflect on our hopes, goals, wishes, dreams, and religion. But things we keep to ourselves, things we hold within our minds, things that stay in the private places of our hearts— these things can quickly pass through our fingers. Maybe you have already experienced that.

Think of marriage. Why is a wedding ceremony necessary? Why not just run off in the night and live together? Wouldn't it be easier if people simply moved in together? No fuss. No muss. And a lot less expensive.

And yet, from generation to generation, people have demanded a ceremony, a public event to confirm the marriage. Why? Perhaps recent research points to an answer.

Studies conducted in Sweden and North America show that couples who live together for a time before making a formal commitment through marriage have a difficult time staying together. More often than not, they get a divorce. Further, the research shows that couples who take marriage vows first—before they move in together—are much more likely to stay married.

What's the explanation? It is that public commitments are stronger than private wishes. Public commitments carry the weight of society and the strength of community. If I tell myself I'll do something and then decide not to do it, I can always convince myself it was fine to change my mind.

But if I tell my wife I'll be home at a certain time or promise someone I'll attend a certain meeting, and I don't keep my word, I let many people down. Their stake in my life holds me to my word.

That's why marriage is a public act. Yes, it's based on private love. But the strength of that love needs public endorsement, public encouragement, public affirmation. That's also why we wear wedding rings—to tell others about the vows we've taken and to declare publicly the parameters of our social lives.

Apply this illustration to faith. Why should anyone have to know that I believe? Why should I make a public declaration of my faith? Because my faith is made meaningful when I declare it, share it, and call on others to affirm it with me.

Faith that would grow strong must be a public faith. Is yours?

∾

Thank you, God, for not being ashamed to call me your child.
Forgive me for slipping you in through the back door of my
heart and calling on you only in the privacy of my heart.
Let me come out of the closet with my faith, and let it
grow strong and broad and true! Amen.

Faith Is Promissory

Read Genesis 17:1-27

*"You must keep my covenant, you and your descendants after
you for the generations to come."*
—Genesis 17:9

Faith that would become stronger must become not only a public faith, but a faith that makes commitments. Commitments are tough for us to cope with because we love freedom. We crave it. We don't want government to restrict us. We don't want our parents to be too strict. We don't want our jobs to consume us. We want to be free!

But what is freedom? What does it mean to be free?

Usually freedom means throwing off our bonds and fetters, tearing down the walls that might close us in. It means taking hold of our own destinies, owing nothing to anyone, standing tall at the helm of our ship.

But liberty, by itself, cannot hold our lives together. It can't steer us or shape us. It can't give us purpose or direction. Liberty merely opens the gate; if there's nothing beyond the gate, we stand there staring out into the void. We may end up destroying ourselves by trying to go in too many directions without a purpose.

Listen to this suicide note left by a young woman who had kept herself free by moving from lover to lover, throwing off all restraints: "I am killing myself because I have never sincerely loved any human being all my life."

She was free! A free spirit, freely giving herself in free relationships. But liberty alone can never give us meaning in life. Freedom opens the door for us, but faith gives us direction when we walk out into the open spaces of our lives.

Abraham had to learn that. The early chapters of Genesis document a series of promises that God made to Abraham, making him truly free. Interestingly, every time God opened a door, Abraham went wandering by himself and lost his sense of purpose. In Genesis 12, God promised him a homeland, but when the famines came, he ran off to Egypt. In Genesis 15, God promised him a son, but Abraham schemed with a younger woman to find an heir.

God repeats these promises to Abraham in Genesis 17, this time going a step further. God challenges Abraham: "If you really believe that I'm

God, if you believe I can keep my word, then it's time for you to turn your faith into a promise. *You* do something to show that you belong to me. Cut the skin of your flesh, and remind yourself of where you got your identity!"

Do you see what God was doing? God didn't want Abraham to hurt, and he wasn't just out to see blood. God wanted Abraham to take hold of his faith for his own sake. Faith had to be Abraham's promise as well as God's, or it would never stick.

Before I met my wife, I had terminated every significant dating relationship I'd had. It happened easily. I'd watch the relationship grow, but when it was commitment time, I couldn't do it. I couldn't sign my name on the dotted line. I couldn't endorse the check of love. I couldn't make a vow of promise. And in that instant, the relationship was always over.

Now I am married. I'm not sure I could never love another woman as I do my wife. But this I do know: When Brenda and I gave each other a promise the day of our wedding, it changed everything about our relationship. Because of those promises, our love is deeper today than either of us could have known.

Faith is a promise. If it isn't, it dies.

~

Lord, take the pieces of my life and bring them together.
Take my commitments and bind them into a larger
relationship with you. Build my faith from the hesitant
promises I put out today, and help me find my identity
in my loyalty to you. In Christ, Amen.

Faith Is Preventative

Read 2 Timothy 1:3-14

Fan into flame the gift of God.
—2 Timothy 1:6

We have learned that faith is public and promissory. Faith is also preventative.

When Jesus walked the dusty roads of Palestine, many came to him to beg for relief from the troubles that plagued their souls. And he released them. He rescued them. He snatched their spirits from whatever torments of hell they suffered.

But do you remember what he said each time? It was always something like "Go and sin no more" or "Go in peace" or "Go and tell others what great things God has done for you."

Faith, said Jesus, is not only something that helped produce a miracle in your life; faith is also the preventative medicine that will keep many of the things that plagued you from happening again. A healthy spiritual life is far more valuable than an emergency faith; it's a preventative medicine that keeps some of the crises of life at bay.

When Louis Pasteur was researching the deadly anthrax virus, he found that once a cow that had the disease recovered, it could never die from anthrax. It was immune.

Our faith can also develop a kind of immunity. If our faith demonstrates itself in commitment, exercises itself in moral habits, and reaches out for the power offered in Scripture and in the church, then it cannot be easily lost when life gets tough.

That's why we need to make small commitments of faith when we're young. Imagine, as Harry Emerson Fosdick did, that life is a journey down the banks of the Jordan River. At some time before we die, we need to cross the river and take up residence in the Promised Land.

In the church, we often direct attention to the lower end of the river, to the wild surge of waves just before the Jordan empties itself into the Dead Sea. Standing on the banks of the Promised Land, we look across at those who have walked a lifetime on the wrong side. We call out to them, urging them to come into the grace of God before it's too late. Many step into the roaring waters and try to swim. Sometimes they struggle across, nearly exhausted by the effort. Sometimes they don't make it. They get lost among the waves, and the waters close in around them. Their hands reach out for help, but it appears to be too late.

But people can easily cross the Jordan earlier than that. They can cross midstream, where the current is weaker. They can even wade across near its source at the Sea of Galilee, where the waters are shallow and trickle slowly.

People who cross the river near its source are like those who make early commitments of faith, who are drawn to a life of faith by the firm hands of parents, teachers, and friends. Isn't it wonderful that they can now walk for a lifetime on the shores of the Promised Land and know faith's preventative power during the rough times?

Have you stepped across the waters yet? It's the best thing you could do for your faith!

$\sim$

Precious Lord, take my hand. Lead me on, help me stand.
When the darkness appears and the night draws near, when
the day is past and gone, at the river I stand—guide my
feet, hold my hand. Take my hand, precious Lord.
Lead me home. Amen.

MEDITATION 35

Make Me a Captive, Lord!

Read Psalm 139:1-18, 23-24

Search me, O God, and know my heart.
—Psalm 139:23

When Michelangelo was young, he felt trapped by the demands and pressures of his family. They wanted to repress him, to hold his creativity and energy in check. In fact, they wanted him to become a banker or businessman.

When he spoke to his family about painting, they beat him. "Fool!" they said as the whip hit his back. "What kind of profit is there in such things?"

How he craved freedom! How he longed for the day when the door of this family prison would swing open and he could walk the streets of the city on his own terms. Finally he grabbed his destiny and pulled himself to freedom—he ran away from home.

What did freedom mean to him? Listen to the words recorded by his biographers: "Now at last I am free! Now at last I can give myself to beauty and to art!"

Freed to serve! Liberated to be once again enslaved, but this time by a vision and a power much greater than himself. Beauty was the ordering principle of his life. It was the faith he clung to when he lay on his back, cooped and cramped, beneath the ceiling of the Sistine Chapel, where he painted the magnificent sweep of human history.

We also have things we long to be freed from: disease, addictions, repressive relationships, and the like. But if we don't have other commitments to replace the things that bind us—as Michelangelo did—we are in danger of floundering through life adrift.

I'll never forget the first funeral I conducted as a young pastor. It was for an eighty-six-year-old man who had been baptized as a baby and had known about God all his life. He wanted so much to believe that God loved him. But he was never able to bring himself to publicly profess his faith.

On his deathbed he cried like a baby, wanting some assurance that God would take him into the everlasting kingdom. His family surrounded him. They knew that God loved him. They knew that their Pa and Opa was going to heaven. They saw the grace of God in his life. But he, of all people, didn't know it. He, of all people, missed the joy of God's grace. He, of all people, went to his grave a restless spirit.

Why? Because even though God had taken hold of his life, the man had never taken hold of his faith in God. You can't affirm a contract without signing on the dotted line. You can't cash a check without endorsing it and taking it to the bank. And you can't make your faith vital and alive without deepening it through the personal attachments of commitment and devotion.

In the words of the minister George Matheson,

> Make me a captive, Lord,
> and then I shall be free;
> force me to render up my sword,
> and I shall conqueror be.
>
> I sink in life's alarms
> when by myself I stand;
> imprison me within thine arms,
> and strong shall be my hand.

Search me, O God, and know my heart; test me and know my anxious thoughts. See if there is any offensive way in me, and lead me in the way everlasting! Amen.

Week 6
Appearing as
Christian as We Truly Are

Mine is a family of book lovers. Early on, my wife and I encouraged our daughters to read and bought them books we thought they'd enjoy. It was no surprise to us that in their younger years the girls chose a book by the look of its cover. But as they grew to love the quality of the stories they read, the appearance of a book became less important. Now they understand that "you can't judge a book by its cover."

English is full of proverbs like that—still waters run deep; beauty is only skin deep; looks can be deceiving; good things come in small packages. We learn quickly to distrust appearances, because too often they don't tell the whole story.

Still, it's nice when the cover of a book is of the same wonderful quality as that of the story inside. I have some leather bound, gold-embossed books that I appreciate as much for their intelligent construction as for their inspiring character.

I know some people like that too, and they're wonderful.

A Dirty Word

Read Matthew 23:13-32

"Woe to you, . . . you hypocrites!"
—*Matthew 23:13*

Once when my wife and I were in a shoe store, the owner told us about his terrific line of quality footwear. "Best in the world," he said. "Better than any of the competition. You can't find the same quality anywhere else."

Then I mentioned another product line, and he said quietly, "Oh, that's something I'd like to sell too." He shook his head back and forth slowly and continued, "But then I'd have to talk both ways at the same time, wouldn't I? And nobody likes to deal with somebody who does that."

He was right, of course. Nobody likes a person who talks two ways at the same time. The ancient Romans had a god named Janus, whom they pictured with two faces peering in opposite directions. For them Janus was a good god. In fact, they called him the god of gates and doorways, because he could look inside and outside at the same time. They also made Janus the god of the New Year, since he could look back at the past and forward to the future at the same time. We still pay lip service to Janus by calling the first month of the year *January*.

But the man in the shoe store was right. We're not Roman gods. We can't get away with looking in two directions at the same time. In fact, we have taken Janus's name and made it an ugly, unbecoming word in the English language. Today if you call someone Janus-faced, you are declaring him a deceiver, a con artist, a two-faced hypocrite.

Nobody likes a Janus. Nobody appreciates a two-faced person. We can put up with a lot of things, but we don't have patience with hypocrisy.

Nor should we. Our Lord Jesus himself saved his most biting words of condemnation for the Pharisees and teachers of the law, who took the heart out of their religion by turning things good and right and honorable into the sham of hypocrisy. He even called them "white-washed tombs"—pretty and shiny on the outside, but stinking with rottenness and decay within.

Hypocrisy leaves a bad taste in our mouths, especially where religion is concerned. I'll never forget the scene in one of Tennessee Williams's plays that describes a preacher. The man dresses like a king. His words are smooth and enticing. He wears a big smile. But Williams says the preacher's smile is "as sincere as a bird call blown on a hunter's whistle."

That's a picture of hypocrisy at its worst, and religion that puts on a face like that deserves to be run out of town.

But hypocrisy happens even in the best Christian homes and communities. In fact, hypocrisy often grows best there, where the groundwork of authentic religion is laid so well. Precisely where grace grows best, so does hypocrisy.

Professor Edward Dowey of Princeton Theological Seminary explained it this way. Suppose that as I walk down the street today, I chance to smile at someone out of a warm and caring heart. To my delight, she smiles back. When I pass her tomorrow, I'll smile again. But tomorrow will I smile because I am moved by joy or because I think I can get her to reward me with another smile? "Today's grace," he said, "becomes tomorrow's law."

And that's the beginning of hypocrisy.

~

God, I delight to live my faith to the fullest. But do I portray myself with godly graces because they overflow from my heart, or am I acting like a Christian because I know that others will commend me for it? Search me out, and help me to live an authentic life. Amen.

Two Kinds of Hypocrisy

Read Matthew 7:15-20; 5:13-16

"By their fruit you will recognize them."
—Matthew 7:20

Years ago, I had a friend who didn't go to church. He was open to "religion," and we often talked about God and the Bible and the church, but every time I invited him to come with me on a Sunday morning, he declined. He was always polite, but he was also firm.

He had reasons, he said. And one day, during one of our relaxed, friendly conversations—and after a lot of coaxing—his reasons came out. He used to work for a member of our congregation, he said, who often talked with him about religion. But he saw the way the man mistreated his wife and abused his children. He watched the shady practices that slipped in with the fellow's business deals.

My friend was turned off. If that kind of behavior is what the church was all about, he didn't want any part of it. And he was right. Hypocrisy is a dirty word that kills the message of the gospel.

But there are two kinds of hypocrites in our world and in the church. If the first kind of hypocrite, like the businessman, pretends to be more than he is, the second pretends to be less than he really is. Jesus refers to both kinds in the Sermon on the Mount.

Here's a good tree, he says, a tree that has what it takes to be something in the orchard of life. But when people look at it, says Jesus, and look under the branches, they shake their heads sadly and walk away. Why? Because the tree has no fruit. The tree is less than it should be. It's a hypocrite of the second kind because it pretends to be something less significant than its heart says it should be.

Or, says Jesus, here's a man who lights a lamp on a dark night. Then, because everything around him is dark, he takes the bright lamp and hides it under his bushel basket. That man is a hypocrite, too, just like the Pharisees who paraded through the streets of Jerusalem blowing their trumpets, shouting their prayers, and thanking God for their righteousness!

Let your light shine, says Jesus. Let your fruit grow! Let your Christianity be seen! This command challenges the hypocrisy within us that too often makes us less than we need to be in our world. It says, "Act as Christian as you truly are. Be in your life what God has made you in your heart. Let your conviction grow strong in the fruit of your daily activities."

We have a tendency to hide our Christian faith, because we're afraid of the comments of others. We want to go with the flow and mix with the crowd. The pressures to conform with the mindset of the world around us are great.

But hiding our faith is hypocrisy—just as hypocritical as the polished smile of the fake preacher or the trumpeted piety of the Pharisee. And when we play that game of hypocrisy too long, the quality of our faith can diminish.

~

Father, we learn early in life to play wonderful games.
Help us to know the difference between the games of sport
and the games of hypocrisy. In our relationships with you
and with the world around us, let the convictions of our
hearts ring true and genuine. Help us to be the best we
can be in our faith. Amen.

The World Needs It

Read Galatians 5:16-26

Live by the Spirit.
—Galatians 5:16

Ask yourself these questions: What lifestyle do I seek from my neighbor? What kind of people do I truly desire to know? What qualities do I look for in a friend?

Greed or arrogance? No. Insensitivity, lawlessness, destructiveness, disregard for others? You know you stay away from people with those qualities.

Try to summarize, for a minute, the kind of people you need to know to make life bearable and pleasant, the kind of people you desire to have in your community. Here's what you'll find: you want a friend who loves you. You want to be among those who laugh with gusto and joy. You want a political leader who can bring peace instead of war. You appreciate a neighbor who is patient with you. You want your roommate who is kind, especially when you're hurting.

Do you see where this is leading? You're looking for what Paul described as the fruit of the Spirit. You're looking for persons and nations and societies that bear themselves with love, joy, peace, patience, kindness, goodness, faithfulness, gentleness, and self-control. You're looking for people who act as Christian as they truly are!

When the Danish novelist Georg Brandes was a young man, he looked up to Henrik Ibsen. Ibsen was much older than Brandes, but he took notice of the young writer. Once Brandes asked the famous dramatist for help and encouragement.

Ibsen wrote a long letter in response, sharing this advice: If you want to serve your world, you have to look inside first. You have to find out what you're made of. You have to mine the depths of your own heart.

Then you have to be true to yourself, letting your faith shine for others. Said Ibsen, "There is no way in which you can benefit society more than by coining the metal you have in yourself."

He was right. No Christian can bring anything of true value to his world by putting on airs, by denying the grace of God within, or by keeping the power of the Spirit locked up. Pious hypocrisy is of no benefit to the world.

We're always eager to talk about the worst in society—corruption, greed, shams, materialism. Are we also eager to talk about the best of God within us? The strength of those who hold weak hands and trembling knees? The generosity of those who break bread with the poor? The courage of those who say "No" when the rage of the world says "Yes" or of those who by faith in God say "Yes" when the scoffers of the world say "No"?

What does your world need? Have you heard its voice? Then begin again today to appear as Christian as you truly are!

~

Lord, let me hear the voice of the world around me today.
Let me hear the cries for love and joy and peace. Let me feel
the need for patience, kindness, and goodness. Let me sense
the prayers of those who ask for faithfulness, gentleness,
and self-control. And then, Lord, let me live in ways
that give them my best. For Christ's sake, Amen.

Our Lord Needs It

Read Luke 6:43–49

*"Why do you call me, 'Lord, Lord,'
and do not do what I say?"*
—*Luke 6:46*

When Jesus was on the cross, soldiers approached him with swords and spears. They wanted to hurry death along, to finish the job, to make sure that the bodies of those being hanged could be taken down by nightfall.

The two criminals next to Jesus were still alive, so the soldiers broke their legs, knowing the trauma would kill them.

When they came to Jesus, they saw he was already dead. To confirm his death, they thrust a spear into his side, spilling his blood. Throughout centuries of speculation about the exact cause of Jesus' death, some Christians have said that Jesus died of a broken heart.

That's a sickly sweet, overly dramatic explanation—rather like a soap opera, isn't it?

But is it very far from the truth? Luke painted a vivid picture of Jesus looking down on Jerusalem from the Mount of Olives. Jesus cried the tears of a broken heart. He spoke to the city through sobs of grief, shaking his head over its spurning of his love, its rejection of his grace, its callousness.

Might we not say with dignity that our Lord died on Calvary of a broken heart? But if our Lord died of a heart broken by those who spurned him, he also lives today in the hearts of those who radiate his kindness, goodness, and beauty.

Think of Zacchaeus's face the day he found Jesus. Imagine the look in his eye as he told of the change in his heart. Recall what he said he would do because Jesus had come to dine with him, because Jesus had spoken to him about the kingdom of heaven, because Jesus had taught him what it means to say, "Lord! Lord!" Zacchaeus's newfound faith transformed his life. Jericho became a better place because Zacchaeus learned how to speak with actions as well as words. He began to appear on the outside as he truly was inside.

Faith did not come easily to Robert Louis Stevenson. As a young man, he threw stones at the hypocrisy of the church. He trumpeted his atheism in the streets, disgusted with the simplistic religious talk of others.

But Stevenson realized that he, too, could become a hypocrite—an atheistic hypocrite—by writing God too easily out of his life. He could turn away from a church that said too much and did too little, to a life that simply said far too little.

Realizing this danger, he went to the Samoan islands to examine his spirituality. He had spent his life building birds' nests, he wrote, and it was time to be true to himself, to find out what was inside, to build what he could from the resources of his heart.

What did he find? Later, in a letter to his father, he wrote, "No man can achieve success in life until he writes in the journal of his life the words, 'Enter God! Enter God!'"

~

Lord, let me call you by name in my prayers and live you by grace in the activities of my life. Let the words of my heart and the meditations of my daily activities be the same cry of faith. In Christ, Amen.

My Own Faith Needs It

Read Matthew 7:24-27

"Everyone who hears these words of mine and puts them into practice is like a wise man who built his house on the rock."
—Matthew 7:24

Caesar Augustus was the mighty Roman emperor who brooded over the world at the time of Jesus' birth. Did you ever hear the story of how he achieved his position of power?

If you had seen what he looked like, you never would have expected him to gain an exalted position in society. Here is how those who knew him described him: He is quite short; he has such sensitive skin that he dares not be out in the sun too long—and never without his head covered; he walks with a limp; his right hand fails him from time to time, so he rarely uses it; bladder stones cause him daily pain; he doesn't sleep well; he catches cold easily; and horseback riding tires him, so he is often carried to the battlefield on a litter.

Can you imagine a man bearing that description becoming the great Caesar Augustus?

Part of his secret lies in an event that occurred when he was a young boy. One day he visited the well-known astrologer and fortune-teller Theogenes. When Theogenes read the boy's horoscope, he was so impressed with its prophesy that he fell on his face and worshiped him.

You and I may not believe in astrology, but Caesar Augustus did. All throughout the struggles of his life, he lived as if this prophecy were true. And eventually it became true.

This story of Caesar Augustus is similar in some ways to the story Jesus told about the wise and foolish builders. Just as the efforts of Caesar Augustus determined his future, so the builders' workmanship determined the nature of their homes. The foolish builder's home looked fine from the outside, but the builder didn't apply his knowledge when he built it. When the storm winds blew, it tumbled in a heap of rubbish. It was false. Its appearance was meaningless because its character was hollow. And that, said Jesus, was the Pharisees' problem as well.

If the foolish builder's house was false, the wise builder's was as honest as polished wood. Through a lifetime of hard work, he built a home and a reputation that were genuine and true, like a piece of wood that is solid to the core.

The point of Jesus' story is this: a faith that seeks to be strong must be used and exercised and stretched. If faith isn't put into practice, it becomes hollow; it eventually becomes no faith at all.

Charles Darwin grew up in a Christian home, yet later in life he rejected Christianity's hold on him. How did this loss of faith happen? Here's the explanation from his autobiography: "I gradually came to disbelieve in Christianity. . . . Disbelief crept over me at a very slow rate, but at last it was complete. The rate was so slow that I felt no distress."

Darwin's words could have fallen from the pages of many diaries. His experience is the same as many in the church who lose their faith. They lose it because they don't use it. Because they never do anything with it. Because they have become less than they truly are.

What are you doing with who you are? Are you exercising your faith? Does it show?

~

Every day, Lord, I'm building my future. Let the bricks I lay and the furnishings I use to adorn my life establish a reputation of depth and quality. Let me use my faith as I grow, and let it grow with me. Amen.

Habits of the Heart

Read 1 Corinthians 9:24-27

Everyone who competes in the games goes into strict training.
—*1 Corinthians 9:25*

Habits are hard to break, but they are just as hard to make. One habit that demands a lifetime of practice is the habit of a deep faith, a firm belief, and a Christianity that runs true.

Some people believe it is valuable to "sow wild oats" when we're young or to do something just to "get it out of our system." And maybe we do need to experience superficial things in order to find our way to things that truly matter. But we need to be careful, because habits are hard to break, and habits of shallow living are just as hard to break as are habits of deep living.

Paul knew the value of developing the habit of faith. He practiced his faith like an athlete training for a sporting event. He exercised it like he exercised his body. He dug his faith into his life like a soldier digging his sense of duty into his muscles. If he didn't do that, Paul said, there was a good chance his faith would fail him.

Practice is necessary in any area of life in which we want to excel. A woman once rushed up to the great pianist Arthur Rubinstein after a brilliant performance. "Oh, Mr. Rubinstein," she gushed, "I'd give anything to be able to play like you do!" Rubinstein was honest in his reply. "No you wouldn't," he said, "because you didn't!"

The same lesson applies to faith. Have you ever known a person of great faith who didn't have to fight for it, struggle with it, and grow it out of the difficulties of her life?

During World War II, many members of the Lutheran church in Germany lost their faith because Hitler seduced them into ways of living that kept them from practicing their faith. But there was one man whom Hitler couldn't seduce. His name was Martin Niemöller. During World War I, Niemöller was a great hero in the German military. But during the Second World War, he refused to bow to the authorities. He was marching to a different drumbeat. And march he did. When Hitler couldn't make him change his tune, couldn't bring him in line with the Nazis' brutal policies, he had him thrown into a concentration camp.

Seven years later, when he came out of the camp, this is what he said: "Christianity is not an ethic, nor is it a system of dogmatics, but a living thing." Everyone who saw the fruits of his life knew who he was and where he stood and how he built his reputation.

Sometimes it seems fashionable to downplay our faith, to show ourselves in tune with our world, to treat Christianity flippantly. "Don't become a fanatic," we say. "Don't go overboard with religion. I believe in my heart; just don't ask me to make a big deal of it."

But our faith is a big deal—or it's no deal at all. Our relationship with God is everything or nothing. With Paul, we either develop the habit of a deep faith or we get stuck in the habits of the world.

~

Teach me today, Lord, the drumbeat that guides my life.
Help me to hear the music I've been following, and let
see me its effects on my actions. Let me choose patterns of
behavior that keep me true to your ways and habits of
the heart that build my faith. Amen.

Back to the Basics

Read 2 Peter 1:1-11

Make your calling and election sure.
—2 Peter 1:10

Victor Hugo called his masterpiece *Les Miserables* a religious work. So it is. The story echoes the gospel message at nearly every turn.

The main character, Jean Valjean, has been beaten hard by the cruel twists of fate. He has seen the sham of hypocrisy on all sides. So he casts the name of the Lord to the ground like a curse. What does God know of him, and what does it matter?

Imprisoned for stealing bread to feed his family and resentenced by the vindictive will of his jailer, Jean Valjean finally manages to escape. On his first night of freedom, he stays with a bishop, who treats him well. But behind Jean Valjean's thankful mask is the cunning face of a thief, for the bishop has many valuables.

In the early morning hours, Jean Valjean steals away with some silver plates. And when his suspicious appearance brings him under arrest, he is forced to face the bishop again, charged with new crimes.

Then the miracle of grace occurs. For in Jean Valjean's eyes the bishop sees something that begs forgiveness and hopes for mercy. Instead of taking revenge, the bishop declares that the silver dishes were a gift to Jean Valjean. In fact, he says Jean Valjean forgot to take the two silver candlesticks he had also given him.

In an instant, the bishop declares Jean Valjean innocent and gives him back his life. But with this gift of forgiveness, he commissions Jean Valjean to bring Christ to others. The rest of Jean Valjean's life becomes a testimony of one who is made new in the grace of divine love.

The bishop's love erases all previous encounters with religious hypocrisy.

I know another story about hypocrisy—the story of the Happy Hypocrite. It is about a man who lived a worthless life. He used everything for his pleasure and treated women like toys to break and throw away. One day he met a young woman whose life intrigued him. She was a Christian, and her actions supported her testimony of faith.

In order to have his way with her, the man put on a mask of piety. He went to church with her and pretended to be as sincere as the mask he wore. Soon, he thought, when she trusts me, I'll use her and toss her on the heap of my conquests.

Then something happened that he hadn't counted on—he fell in love. He began to truly appreciate and adore this woman. Always he kept his mask in place. Always he played the part of her righteous friend. And gradually she fell in love with him, too. Incredible as it seemed to him, they got married, and he found himself enjoying the role of godly husband.

But one day one of his former consorts found out who he was. She was livid. He had used and tossed her aside, and she wanted revenge. She met with him privately, telling him she would reveal the hideous truth to his wonderful wife. She'd crush him just the way he had crushed her so many years before.

She rushed at him to snatch the mask from his face and reveal the ugly man beneath. But when the mask fell away, the face behind it looked just like the pious mask. Love had changed this cruel man's heart; the habits of his life had molded his face to fit his mask of righteousness.

When Love has its way with us, our face and our life will find its shape in him.

~

Dear Lord and Father of mankind,
forgive our foolish ways;
re-clothe us in our rightful mind,
in purer lives thy service find,
in deeper reverence, praise. Amen.

Week 7
Hearing the Melody
Above the Harmony

Throughout the second half of this century, composers have experimented with new sounds in music. One musician opens a piano and hits the wire strings with a variety of objects. Another searches for the most discordant sounds he can produce on his synthesizer. A third programs her computer to select random pitches and randomly fuses them together.

Audiences won't tolerate these forms of music long. There's something irrepressible about a clean melody that carries a continuing theme. Bach, Beethoven, and Tchaikovsky knew that. Folk artists thrive on that. Musicians who cater to the burgeoning children's market make a grand living on that.

Music is not merely a set of random pitches thrown together. The best pieces have a clear melody that defines a mood, supports an idea, transforms a vision, or deepens a feeling. Without harmony, a melody may quickly run thin. But harmony never works without a melody stating the theme.

A Great Noise

Read Ezra 3:7-13

---

*No one could distinguish the sound of the shouts of joy from
the sound of weeping, because the people made so much noise.*
—Ezra 3:13

I enjoy singing. Over the years, I've sung in a variety of choirs. Even when I'm alone I sometimes sing. Once in a while I'll put some of my favorite music on the stereo, turn the volume way up, and sing along at the top of my voice.

Then I know how cruel my voice really is, because our three daughters come running with their hands over their ears, shouting, "Daddy! Turn the music down! It's too loud!"

One rural church choir I know of has a problem finding tenors. Sopranos are a dime a dozen; altos come to practices freely; even basses aren't hard to find; but there's a dearth of tenors. It's as if a virus came through one year and carried all tenors away.

One season this choir had only two tenors. They were pretty good, mind you, and in tandem they made a joyful noise. They were usually able to balance out the other parts reasonably well. But one piece of music didn't work for them, because it gave the tenor section the melody. As hard as the two tenors tried, they couldn't prevent their voices from being drowned out by the others. When the choir performed that piece, the audience didn't understand it, because it lacked the element that makes a song live—a melody.

Ezra 3 tells a similar story. When the foundations of the temple were being relaid in Jerusalem, the returned exiles threw a party, knowing their work was accomplishing something wonderful. But as some voices rose in songs of praise, others rose with a cry of mourning for what was and would never be again. From a distance, the joyful tunes could not be distinguished from the sounds of weeping. There was a lot of music, but where, exactly, was the melody?

It must have been a strange sound for the peoples scattered around Jerusalem to hear. What were these Israelites up to? Were they having a party or a funeral?

In reality, there were mixed emotions in the Israelite community. Some marveled that God had brought them back from captivity and had given them the strength to lay the foundations of God's house again. Others, however, remembered the past—the greatness of David's kingdom and the glory of Solomon's temple. They viewed this paltry imitation under rather pernicious political circumstances as a display of poverty rather than of righteous might.

Are we weak or strong? Is God with us or has he left us? Do good intentions overcome lackluster achievements? These were the uncertainties behind the cacophony the Israelites produced that day.

Shall we read in these eclectic emotions faith or doubt?

Because of the uncertainty of the human heart, this question applies not only to the situation recorded in Ezra 3; it speaks to all of us. Our moods are rarely unmixed, and amidst the sounds we make, the melody doesn't always come through.

∿

Lord, sometimes it's difficult for people to hear the melody of my life because I'm not sure what tune I want to sing. Help me to sort out my mixed emotions, and bring them together in a sense of peace that reflects your work within me. In Christ, Amen.

Many Faces

Read Psalms 42 and 43

Why are you downcast, O my soul?
—Psalm 42:5

A young girl came downstairs for breakfast one morning singing a delightful tune. Her face was as bright and cheery as could be.

As she rushed into the kitchen, she saw a glum scowl on her mother's face. "Mommy," she said, "you're sad this morning, aren't you?"

"No, honey," replied her Mom, looking down at her. "I'm not sad; I'm happy!"

"Well," said her daughter, "you'd better tell your face, because it still thinks you're sad."

So it is with us, many times. We don't know whether we are happy or sad. Look, for example, at these Psalms of the Sons of Korah. Is the person singing them happy or sad? On the one hand he speaks of tears and anger, doubt and difficulty. He's haunted and taunted by those who hate him and his silent God.

But on the other hand he speaks of joy and faith, love and friendship. Happy melodies compete with dissonant chords.

I think people love Psalms 42 and 43 precisely because they express the spectrum of our emotions. We appreciate the mixed messages of these psalms because our own experience is mixed. The harmonies that ring through these psalms reflect the emotions that swing through our souls.

In his poem "Augeries of Innocence," the English poet William Blake expressed this truth powerfully. He said,

> Man was made for Joy & Woe
> And when this we rightly know
> Thro the World we safely go
> Joy & Woe are woven fine
> A Clothing for the Soul divine.

Every day our soul changes its clothes. Every hour, sometimes. Some of us, in our steady predictability, may wear only a few garments. But others have a huge wardrobe, and we fling our moods and emotions this way and that, dressing our soul each moment with a new face, a different mood.

A few years ago, Dr. Willard Gaylin wrote a book about moods called *Feelings* (Harper & Row, 1979). In it he says that compressed between the two poles of our hearts—the pole of feeling good and the pole of feeling bad— are "all the joys of heaven and all the anguish of hell." He says our feelings are "slippery things;" they're hard to grasp, hard to analyze, hard to separate from one another.

These Psalms illustrate Gaylin's point. The moods run together. The emotions stack themselves first in this corner and then in that. The feelings slip from the shadows into the sunlight and then back again.

The words of the old spiritual put it well:

> Sometimes I'm up, sometimes I'm down
> Oh, yes, Lord!
> Sometimes I'm almost to the ground
> Oh, yes, Lord!

Those are the faces of our lives, aren't they? And they have a habit of tripping us up when we least expect it.

~

My life is complex, Lord. I'm thankful that Jesus is human like me, because he understands the mixture of moods and emotions that put a different face on me twenty times a day. Actually, I'm thankful, too, that my life is so wonderfully complex. It makes me more interesting, don't you think? Amen.

MEDITATION 45

An Upside-Down World

Read 1 Kings 18:22-24, 36-39; 19:1-5

"I have had enough, LORD."
—1 Kings 19:5

Elijah was drained, tired of the swinging emotions that had followed him throughout his ministry. I know what he went through. I never had trouble sleeping before I became a pastor. I could usually lie down at night, make my peace with God, and fall quickly into slumber.

But life is different now. I remember my first year in the ministry. Early in the morning I'd meet with a young man from my congregation—a truck driver—for prayer. We'd spill our hearts to one another and talk about our spiritual struggles.

Then I'd visit one of our senior citizens for morning coffee. She'd relate her joys and sorrows and update me on the comings and goings of her children and grandchildren. Sometimes we'd laugh and other times we'd cry.

When I went to the post office to pick up the mail, I'd usually encounter a group gossiping about the best and worst in the community. Sometimes someone would vent his anger, and the daggers that pierced my soul would remain even after I walked away.

Off to the hospital in the afternoon. I'd talk with a teenager who had anorexia nervosa, an elderly man dying of cancer, and a mother with her new baby. My emotions would spin round and round, following the tune playing in each room.

At night we'd have a church meeting. Each person had opinions, often packaged in deeply-rooted feelings. Strong words were spoken, and sentiments ran high.

By the time I got home at night, my emotions were fully charged. In my heart they taunted and challenged one another. And my brain would keep whirling while my body cried out for sleep.

We like to think that we're rational beings, ruled by reason, controlled by knowledge, and steadied by logic. We think we live by our brains. If we understand something, that knowledge will determine our actions.

But that's not the way it really is. Most of the time, whether we want to or not, we live by emotions and moods. The feelings of the heart prove themselves mightier than the logic of the brain.

In England, the story is told of a man who went to the doctor because he was depressed and emotionally disturbed. He couldn't cope with life. He was contemplating suicide. He had trouble sleeping at night.

The doctor gave him a complete physical examination. Nothing showed up; there was nothing physically wrong with him. So the doctor decided to prescribe a different kind of medicine. "Go to the theater at Covent Garden," he said, "and take in the show of Grimaldi the Clown. Get yourself a good laugh. That's what you need!"

The man stared at him and shuddered. "But, doctor," he said. "I'm Joseph Grimaldi. I'm the Clown of Covent Garden!"

I understand his problem. At church one Sunday one of our elders saw a young woman crying with me in agony. After she left, the elder came and put his arm around me. "Who pastors the pastor?" he asked.

I was emotionally drained, the highs of worship and lows of that young woman's pain tugging at my soul. I knew there was no good answer to the elder's probing question. But I also knew, like Elijah, that during times of emotional turmoil, it's sometimes okay to let go and rest in the arms of someone who dares to ask that question.

~

Nothing is more demanding, Lord, than the mighty tug-of-war between our different emotional states. When we have been bandied about by emotional concerns, let us find the arms of caring that would allow us to drift quietly away and rest awhile apart from the turmoil of our souls. Amen.

The Dark Side

Read Psalm 22:1-21

My strength is dried up.
—*Psalm 22:15*

Hebrew is a descriptive language. The Hebrew word that we usually translate *despair* implies the picture of a person crouching down and rolling up, like a child sleeping in the fetal position. This is a normal posture for a child, but when you go to the psychiatric ward of a hospital and see a grown man folded up like that, you feel the agony of his despair.

You know that he can't talk himself out of his despair. He hasn't the strength to step from the shadows into the sunlight, from his inner turmoil into peace and rest.

John Knox, the great reformer of the Church of Scotland, once wrote a pathetic prayer entitled "John Knox with Deliberate Mind to his God." His theme is summarized in a single line: "Now, Lord, put an end to my misery."

Or take Martin Luther, who stood resolutely before Emperor Charles V at the Concordat in Worms, and boldly cried, "Here I stand. I can do nothing else. God help me!" The same man wrote these words in a letter to a friend: "Old, decrepit, lazy, worn-out, cold, and now one-eyed, I write, my Jacob, I who hoped there might at length be granted to me, already dead, a well-earned rest." These are the emotions of a tired man, an old man, a man worn out by life's emotional battles.

"A sigh," says the Talmud, "can break a man in two." In our dark days, during times of sighing, our terrible experiences can even rob us of our faith. Or so it seems.

At age sixty-eight, Dr. Joseph Parker, the famous English preacher, wrote that he had never doubted God. He'd never disbelieved. He'd never felt the cold washes of a trembling faith. But a year later, when he wrote again about his life, his wife of five decades had just died. All the theological arguments he knew so well couldn't touch his wasting spiritual beliefs. "In that dark hour," he said, "I almost became an atheist."

Read his words, and compare them with the words of Psalm 22: "God had set his foot upon my prayers and treated my petitions with contempt. If I had seen a dog in such agony as mine, I would have pitied and helped

the dumb beast; yet God spat upon me and cast me out as an offence—
out into the vast wilderness and the night black and starless."

Can't you see the dark harmonies of his soul drowning out what he
thought was the melody of his life?

In *Mere Christianity*, C. S. Lewis wrote that when a person finally
makes a firm intellectual choice for the Christian faith, it won't be another
mental argument that defeats him. It will be the emotions that burst out
when he hears a piece of bad news, or the feelings that run wild when his
coworkers make fun of his faith, or the moods that wash over him when
trouble strikes him down. That's how he'll lose his faith.

How true that is. Have you been there, too?

~

*Sometimes we see you at the cross, Lord Jesus, and hear
you cry, lost and alone, isolated from your father in the
swirling of the dark side. Sometimes, Lord, we're there
with you. Sometimes the shadows of our souls smother
the bright lights of your love. You know what we're
going through, because you cried David's prayer, too.
Shelter us when we meet you there again. Amen.*

Our Truest Selves

Read Psalm 27

My heart says of you, "Seek his face!"
Your face, LORD, I will seek.
—*Psalm 27:8*

What do we do when the darker harmonies of our souls torment us?
What can we do when loneliness, guilt, anxiety, discouragement, anger,
inferiority, and emptiness tear at our hearts, making a mockery of our
faith?

We can ask ourselves a question. We need to look at the many faces of
our moods and ask, "When am I *most* myself?"

That's a hard question to ask, because we tend to think that our truest
self is represented by the emotion that is strongest right now, at this
moment.

But is it? Consider that we really have only two kinds of emotions:
emotions that tear us apart and emotions that pull us together. Emotions
that break us down and emotions that draw us out and make us whole.

David reflects on these two kinds of emotions in Psalm 27. He remembers the joy of worship that used to catch him up in ecstasy. He
recalls the sense of peace that made him strong. He thinks about the
laughter of the community that gave him a sense of belonging. *These* are
the emotions that express the best in him. These are the feelings that re-
store his soul. These are the moods he associates with his faith in God.
That's why, in his darkest hours, his mind has to teach his heart where to
find its melody: "Seek the Lord!" is the cry. He knows that his truest self
is not the emotional doubter, but the worshiper.

Our houses are built with basements, but we don't live in our basements. Tall buildings have deep foundations, but the offices are above
ground level. So too with our lives. We have dark emotions, moody
thoughts. But we don't live in them. That's not where we find our truest
selves. "We live in the heights with Christ," says Paul in the New Testament. We find the best of ourselves in praise and joy and laughter. We
find ourselves in the worship of our God.

When John Bunyan first came to know the Lord, he wrote in his diary,
"I was so taken with the love and mercy of God that I knew not how to

contain myself till I got home. I thought I would have spoken of his love to the very crows that sat upon the ploughed lands before me." Those words reflect Bunyan's truest self.

And later in his life, when his enemies threw him into the Bedford jail and tore at his spirit and played with his psyche, his emotions told him to give up, to end his life.

But then he remembered his family. He remembered his poor blind child. He summoned his courage and told himself that he must not give up; he must keep faith with his family. And in those dark days of imprisonment, Bunyan began to write his spiritual classic *The Pilgrim's Progress*.

If you've read the book, you know that early in his journey of faith, Christian gets stuck in the Slough of Despond. Up to his waist in trouble, stuck in dark emotions, Christian begins to lose his faith in God.

Then someone called Help reminds him of his true identity and pulls him back to the firmness of the road.

~

When my feet are stuck in the muck and my hands are clammy with fear and my knees are about to give out, remind me, Lord, of who I truly am. Remind me of past joys, and lift me again onto the road of my pilgrimage toward you. In Christ, Amen.

Soaring the Song

Read Psalm 30

*You turned my wailing into dancing; you removed my
sackcloth and clothed me with joy, that my heart
may sing to you and not be silent.*
—*Psalm 30:11*

The melody of our lives is not sung by the darkest voices within, but by the brightest and best and most bountiful. "Faith," said Browning, "is my waking life: One sleeps, indeed, and dreams at intervals, we know, but waking's the main point with us." And our waking hours are our best hours, our highest moments, our truest feelings.

Charles Dickens's novel *A Tale of Two Cities* contains the story of a prisoner who had spent most of his life in the Bastille, the great prison of Paris. In the darkness of the dungeon, he cobbled shoes, not knowing day from night.

When he was finally released, he returned to his home in England. But there, in the center of his house, which was flooded with light by large windows, he built a tiny, dark cell of bricks. There he spent his days. When the skies above were sunny and birds sang from every tree, his neighbors could hear the tapping of his hammer as he sat in his narrow cell, comforted by its darkness, smallness, and isolation.

His behavior is not normal. We know it does not reflect the character's truest self. His emotions have taken him captive, even when his body is free. Our hearts cry out to him, "Come outside! Open your eyes to the sunlight. Hear the joy of creation's song. Here is life. Here is faith. Here is God!"

In Psalm 30, the psalmist's enemies challenge him to stay in his dark cell of despair, to hug the walls, to doubt his faith. But he refuses. He will not remain forever in the dark places of the soul. "I will exalt you, O LORD," he cries, "for you lifted me out of the depths and did not let my enemies gloat over me" (v. 1). He has found the doorway to his cell and will not let his darker emotions rob him of his faith.

Someone once took the Old Testament story of Joseph the dreamer—despised by his brothers, thrown into a pit, and sold as a slave—and made it our story. He wrote:

Dreamer of dreams? we take the taunt with gladness,
Knowing that God beyond the years you see,
Has wrought the dreams that count with you for madness
Into the texture of the world to be!

With God's help, we can turn the difficult times of our lives into a song of gladness. Yet many people, said the author Oliver Wendell Holmes, "die with their music still in them." How unfortunate that they never hear their true melody. How sad that their dreams die within because they've never found the doorway to the cathedral of grace, where dark and light are sorted, where sorrow and security are balanced, where doubt and determination are steadied, and where feelings and faith find their proper homes.

If you know the true melody of your life, sing it a little stronger. The life it saves may be your own!

~

Father, long before the worlds existed, you sang the melody of my life. Your song called this world into being, and your voice chanted my soul from slumber into wakeful awareness of your glory. When I slip into the coma of dark moods, shout the melody of your grace from heaven, and let me soar again. Amen.

God's Weavings

Read Romans 8:22-39

In all things God works for the good of those who love him.
—Romans 8:28

Dr. Leslie Weatherhead served as a chaplain with the British army in the Middle East during World War I. There, he says, he watched with fascination as a master craftsman wove colorful Persian rugs in the marketplace.

The loom was made of two poles with threads strung between them. The craftsman stood on one side of the loom, facing the crowds that gathered, and pushed his needles through to the other side.

Behind the rug his young assistants waited. When the master's needle came through, they pulled the thread tight and sent the needle back to the other side. All the while, the master chatted with the crowds, making his work a performance.

What fascinated Weatherhead most was this: sometimes the young assistants pushed the needles back through in the wrong places. The errors were obvious to all in front, a blot on the fine pattern that was developing.

When he first saw this happen, Weatherhead assumed the master would scold the boys and push the needle back, undoing their mistake before continuing to weave his pattern. But he didn't. This man was more than a master craftsman; he was a genius. When the needles came through misplaced and the dark colors seemed to overtake the bright ones in the wrong places, he recreated the pattern. He transformed the dark mistakes into a more brilliant picture.

What a lovely image of the grace of our Master Craftsman, who can create beauty for us in spite of the dark spots in our lives.

Do you remember the words of William Blake?

> Joy & Woe are woven fine
> A Clothing for the Soul divine.

When we remember that, we can rediscover the melody of our lives— not the dark harmonies of pain and despair, real as they are, but the strong melody of grace that brings out the best in us. The Maker of the universe can make that melody the theme of our lives.

The composer Rossini was once commissioned by an opera company to write an aria. The only problem was that the featured soloist, a contralto, could sing only one note with grace and beauty—the middle B-flat. Her voice was made for it. Her middle B-flat was glorious, but any other note she sang came out strained and crude.

Some might face Rossini's task with impatience. After all, this soloist was bound to ruin any piece he wrote. But Rossini was undaunted. He demonstrated his genius by penning a recitative that kept her voice on middle B-flat. All around her voice he wove the rich colors and sounds of the orchestra. And put together, it was a tapestry that glowed with perfection.

After all, the melody was sweet. Its single note kept the harmonies—some dark, some bright—in their best places.

Paul paints a similar picture of God's work in our lives. God provides the melody and makes sure we keep singing it in the midst of all the emotional harmonies that might swirl around us.

Martin Luther put it well in this verse:

> For feelings come, and feelings go,
> And feelings are deceiving;
> My warrant is the Word of God—
> Naught else is worth believing.
> Though all my heart should feel condemned
> For want of some sweet token,
> There is One greater than my heart
> Whose Word cannot be broken.
> I'll trust in God's unchanging Word
> Till soul and body sever:
> For, though all things shall pass away,
> His Word shall stand forever!

~

Teach me, Lord, the sound of your love, and let its tune shape the texture of my soul. When life sends burdens that tilt me off-balance, set my heart straight by singing your melody above the competing harmonies. Take my life and let it be filled with your music! In Christ, Amen.

Week 8
Learning to Ride Again

When we go on a family bike ride, no one thinks much about how we're going to glide along. It happens rather naturally.

But it wasn't always that easy. When our three daughters were learning to ride, they all took a few spills. At one point or another, each of them said, "I'm never going to get on that bike again!" And here we are today, a family of bikers.

Fear can keep us flat-footed. But the promise of greater things teaches us to try again.

Horse Stories

Read Isaiah 31:1-3

Woe to those . . . who rely on horses.
—Isaiah 31:1

My favorite horse story is told by Stanley Wiersma (under his pen name, Sietze Buning) in the book *Purpaleanie*. Here is his description of a nine-year-old boy's experience inspecting horses with his father at a local auction:

We
buying horses
at the sale barn
and passing behind
the long rows
of horses'
rears and
you with
a comment
on each horse:

"Too heavy for work."
"Jittery, he jerked as we walked by."
"Slow. Her head hangs too much."
"Too light. Can't pull."

And then
"This one,
of course,
will have a colt
soon."

"But Dad,
that's a gelding."
"Ain't that rotten?
Poor colt has no way
to get out."

From Purpaleanie *by Sietze Buning,* © *1978. Used by permission of Middleburg Press, P.O. Box 166, Orange City, IA 57041.*

Whenever I picture that scene, I grin from ear to ear!

Everyone who has grown up in a rural community has a few good horse stories like that. I'll never forget the thrill I got from riding our big palomino stallion. That horse could run like the wind. Dad bought it for my younger sister, but it had more power than she could handle. So I always ran it through the open fields to tire it before she rode. I still get shivers thinking about those rides.

My wife has a good horse story, too. She and her brother bought horses one year. The first time she rode, the bridle wasn't fixed quite right. Her horse took off suddenly, and she couldn't control it. It raced through an alley of their feedlot and headed for the gate at the end. Just at the last second, instead of leaping over, it skidded to a stop and almost threw Brenda over the fence.

To this day, Brenda has a healthy fear of horses. She understands the familiar saying, When you are thrown by your horse, the first thing to do is get back in the saddle and conquer your fear.

Fear is the crippler. Fear is the paralyzer. Fear is the thing that keeps a rider on the ground, even when she knows she has the skills to ride.

That's not only true with things equestrian. I know a woman who was attacked and robbed years ago when she was taking a walk. Today she hardly dares step out of her house. She has plenty of opportunities to leave the house, but fear grabs her chest every time she thinks about going out. Fear has built a wall between her and the front door, imprisoning her.

You know similar stories—the man who fears water because he almost drowned once; the woman whose teeth rot because she's afraid of going to the dentist; the man who runs from relationships because someone once crushed his heart. Fear is a barrier. Fear is the barbed wire that holds the soul in check.

Fear exists within the religious dimensions of life, too. Scars of old spiritual hurts can keep our faith from riding again. Maybe you know someone for whom that's the case. Maybe you find it so in your own heart.

~

Lord, our lives are battle-scarred, physically and spiritually.
We carry on our bodies the scars of wounds that ached. But
even more, we carry in our hearts the lingering bruises of
times when we looked but couldn't find you, occasions when
our beliefs let us down. Sometimes we're afraid of you and of
the spiritual dimension of our lives. Steady us with your
patience, and teach us to ride again. In Christ, Amen.

The Accents in Life

Read 1 John 4:17-21

Fear has to do with punishment.
—1 John 4:18

The apostle John speaks of fear in religious terms. Fear is the enemy of faith, he says. Fear is a tool of the devil. Fear is the wall around the mind that wants so desperately to believe.

Maybe you know what he means. I know a businessman who used to belong to a Presbyterian church. For some reason, his relationship with the church soured. Now that he's getting older, though, he thinks about God often and wonders what will happen to him when he dies. Yet he can't bring himself back to church because of that old spiritual skirmish. The scars left by theological wounds still linger years after he received them. He's not sure what he believes anymore.

I know a family who stopped going to church several years ago because they were involved in a controversy in which church members accused one another of thinking and believing falsely. The debate eventually ran its course, but the pain lingers. The family members are afraid of what might happen if they let religion play a large role in their lives once more.

Here's someone else who is afraid of religion. It's a young man whose brother died some years ago. He's afraid now to look God in the face because he doesn't know what he will find—will he see a sadistic monster who plays with young lives? Will he find a stern judge who sentences first and asks questions later?

Fear is a crippler. It binds and enslaves us. It rules over us with a whip. John says fear makes promises we believe: promises of pain, poison, persecution, and punishment.

Fear itself can characterize our faith. Even if we do believe in God, even if we do go to church, a religion of fear can keep us from riding the winds of grace. A religion of fear shouts "No!" so loudly that we can't hear the "Yes!" of God's love. Fear keeps the rider on the ground.

A story told in Scotland illustrates this idea. One of the great churches in Edinburgh was Free Saint George's Church. Alexander Whyte, its preacher, had a powerful pulpit ministry. His sermons roared like fire. His thunder shook the rafters. His congregation sat in quivering silence as he delivered hot, spicy warnings from Scripture.

As the congregation grew larger, the church decided to call a second minister. Young Hugh Black was hired as the junior colleague. Every Sunday, Whyte mounted the pulpit in the morning, Black in the evening. Soon a saying developed about the two: in the morning Whyte black-balled the saints, and in the evening Black whitewashed the sinners. Whyte spoke of the terrors of hell, and Black spoke of the love of God.

Do you know what happened? The congregation in the morning grew smaller, stiffer, and more argumentative, while the congregation in the evening grew larger, more enthusiastic, and more graceful. Whyte built walls of fear, but Black opened the gates of love.

~

Lord, help me today to reflect on what I'm looking for in religion. Have I seen it as a tool of fear, forcing me to toe a certain line? Or have I viewed it as the source of love, drawing me toward things right and good and beautiful? I know that what I see is what I get. And I've had enough of the fear that cripples. Amen.

The Power of Fear

Read Mark 4:35–41

"Why are you so afraid? Do you still have no faith?"
—*Mark 4:40*

If you have been thrown by the horse of your religion, if you have scars from your encounters with the church, if your theology scares you, the challenge of Scripture is this: Get back on the horse; find your way into the saddle again; learn how to ride your religion once more.

How do we do that? We begin, in part, by realizing that faith is more powerful than fear. That's difficult, because fear is a powerful force in our lives. Like a horse that has thrown us, fear towers over us. And well it should, because God has given us the strength of fear to keep us from being destroyed. Fear is the alarm that goes off in our hearts whenever danger threatens. Fear can make us run faster and jump higher than we ever thought possible.

A hunter came back to his camp late at night, clothes in shreds, hair full of brambles, skin cut and bruised. He was carrying a beautiful trophy: a magnificent leopard. As his partner looked the animal over, he said, "I don't see a bullet hole. How did you bag this fellow?"

"Oh, I ran him to death," said the hunter.

"What?" exclaimed his partner. "You can't chase a leopard that fast!"

"Who said anything about chasing?" came the reply. "I was out in front!"

Fear will do that to us, won't it? Fear speeds up our reaction time. It strengthens our muscles. It demands that we run from burning houses. Whenever our senses tell us we're being challenged, our adrenal glands squirt some fear into our system, and our energy level increases. You've probably heard stories of mothers who lifted crashed automobiles to release a trapped child. Fear said, "Get that child out of there," so they did.

But the power of fear can hypnotize us, too. It can stand before us and cast a spell that keeps us from moving. Maybe you've seen a hypnotist at work. She puts a man into a trance and draws a circle around him on the floor. Then she tells him that he can't cross the line—that his feet won't be able to because of the barrier set against him. When she wakes him from his trance, try as he might, he cannot cross that line. The hypnotist's suggestion keeps him pinned.

Jesus knew the hypnotic power of fear, the crippling power of anxiety. That is why he so often tells people not to be afraid. In fact, his command not to fear is recorded more than any other single teaching. The gospels record almost two dozen instances in which Jesus challenged people to give up their fears and to try believing in God again. He said it to Peter. He said it to the ruler of the synagogue when he was told that his little girl had died. He said it to the disciples as a group on a number of occasions. Again and again he said it: "Fear not. Don't be afraid. Only believe." It was even the first thing he said after his resurrection.

If doubt and faith are necessary partners in our hearts, fear and faith are mortal enemies, often locked in combat. Only when we acknowledge that faith is stronger than fear can we climb again into the saddle of our religion and ride the horizons with our God.

∽

Often, Lord, I find myself trapped in fear's web. Let me find the strength of my faith as I listen to the distant call of Jesus: "Fear not. Don't be afraid. Only believe." Amen.

A Greater Power

Read 2 Timothy 1:1-12

For God did not give us a spirit of timidity, but a spirit of power, of love and of self-discipline.
—*2 Timothy 1:7*

Herb Miller once told about a woman struggling through the difficulties of the Great Depression. She went, one morning, to the front desk of an insurance company in Minneapolis. In her hand she carried a worn and yellowed piece of paper, an insurance policy issued many years before.

The woman asked whether she could stop making payments on the policy for a while, since she had run out of money. At first the desk clerk was a bit rude. After all, he got calls like this nearly every day, and he didn't want to be bothered with another one.

But then he took another look at the paper. It was a life insurance policy in a man's name. And it was worth $300,000—right in the middle of the depression!

He rubbed his chin thoughtfully. "This is a pretty valuable policy, ma'am," he said finally. "Have you talked with your husband about it?"

"My husband!" she exclaimed. "He's been dead for three years."

There she was, a woman in poverty, a woman crushed by financial fears. And in her hand she held a piece of paper that could turn her life around.

After telling this story, Miller pointed to the message of Jesus Christ—the message that promises the wealth of grace and the power of God. He said, "Security is not the absence of danger, but the presence of God!"

Fear keeps us clutching at paper, tightfisted and anxious. But faith in God releases to us the power of the kingdom of heaven. Faith in God is greater than any fear that might grip us. Listen again to Paul's words to young Timothy: "For God did not give us a spirit of timidity, but a spirit of power, of love and of self-discipline."

According to one who has counted, the words "Fear not" appear 365 times in Scripture. That's one for every day of the year. And that's probably how often we need to hear our Lord warn us about the mesmerizing power of fear and doubt: "Don't be afraid. Only believe!"

When we clutch at paper hopes, Lord, afraid to let go of the tangible, soothe our spirits with your peace. Allow us to fall back into the strength of your love and care so we can find our faith again. Amen.

Homecoming

Read Luke 15:11-24

". . . lost and . . . found."
—*Luke 15:24*

When a rider is thrown by his horse, fear could keep him down. But a true horseman knows that if he didn't climb into the saddle again, he'd be a poorer person for it. He needs to ride. That's who he is.

Think about that analogy when you read Jesus' story of the prodigal son. The young man left home, kicking his father and brother in the face and turning his back on everything he had made a mess of at home. But moving to the far country didn't satisfy his soul. Eventually, friendless and poor, wallowing with swine, he pictured his old home again.

How often do you think he said to himself, "I should go back to my father"? Probably several times. And just as probably, every time he said it, a voice spoke inside him, saying, "You can't go home. You dare not go home. Your father won't take you in—not after what you did to him. Besides, you don't have the strength or courage to go home again. You don't belong there anymore." It was the voice of Fear.

But you know the end of the story. He did go home again. Why? Because another voice also spoke inside him. It was the voice of Faith, and it said, "Your father loves you!" That's all it said.

Anyone who has drifted into the far country still hears that voice within. Above the mesmerizing eyes and jumbled voices of the hypnotist Fear, whispers another voice—the voice of the Spirit of God, the voice of Faith—saying, "Your Father loves you! Go home to him again!"

When Fear whimpers within, "I can't go back," Faith says: "You can!"

One of Ralph Waldo Emerson's poems puts this way:

> So nigh is grandeur to our dust,
> So near is God to man,
> When Duty whispers low, Thou must,
> The youth replies, I can!

"Even youths," said Isaiah, "grow tired and weary, and young men stumble and fall; but those who hope in the LORD will renew their strength. They will soar on wings like eagles; they will run and not grow weary, they will walk and not faint" (Isa. 40:30-31). They know that the life of fear is so much poorer than the life of faith.

And when they hear the voices of Fear whispering inside, they know that the voice of Faith will follow: "Go home again; your Father loves you!"

~

Lord, let me hear the voices within, and the let the voice of Faith rule over the voice of Fear. Remind me graciously each morning that I can never go so far from you that I am lost forever. Bring me home once more, and teach me to ride with you. In Christ, Amen.

Face to the Son

Read Romans 8:1-17

---

*For you did not receive a spirit that makes you a slave again
to fear, but you received the Spirit of sonship.*
—Romans 8:15

Do you know someone who has left the church? Someone who has allowed fear to dictate the terms of her theology?

I talked to someone like that recently. Over the years I watched his faith shrivel up as he lost his sense of flying with God. Now he stumbles along slowly with his fear. He's not a happy man; fear has drained the joy right out of him.

Singer and songwriter Don Francisco paraphrased Paul's words in Romans 8 as God's tender call to a man like that. Hear the whisper of heaven:

> I know what you've been hearing; I've seen you hide your fears:
> Embarrassed by your weaknesses, afraid to let me near.
> I wish you knew how much I long for you to understand:
> No matter what may happen, Child, I'll never let go of your hand!
>
> The life that I have given you, no one can take away.
> I've sealed it with my Spirit, Blood, and Word.
> The Everlasting Father has made his Covenant with you,
> And he's stronger than the world you've seen and heard!
>
> So don't you fear to show them all the love I have for you.
> And I'll be with you everywhere, in everything you do.
> And even if you do it wrong and miss the joy I've planned,
> No matter what may happen, Child, I'll never let go of your hand!

This is the message that calls our faith to life. No fear in the world could ever promise so much. That's why the purpose and meaning of our lives are not found in doubt or fear, but in faith and flight and the fullness of divine love. We are at our best when we ride in the love of God, when we get back into the saddle of faith and turn our face toward the Son.

When Alexander the Great was a boy, a man from Thessaly brought a horse to his father. The horse was for sale, and it was a raging beauty. No one at court had ever seen a horse so glorious.

King Philip had his grooms test the horse, but they returned discouraged. "The horse is no good," they said. "He's skittish. He's wild. No one will ever tame him."

Philip was about to send the man and his horse on their way when young Alexander stopped him. "Let me try," he said.

Philip was worried. He didn't want the horse to throw his son. But Alexander knew how to coax his father, and Philip finally gave in.

Alexander walked quickly to the horse's head and turned its face toward the sun. He put his mouth to the horse's ears and spoke softly to it. When he got on its back, the horse carried him like an old friend. The two flew together as if they were one.

"How did you do it?" people asked him later.

This was Alexander's secret: "I saw he was afraid of his shadow. So I turned his face to the sun, and I told him I was his friend. And when we rode together, there was nothing to fear."

Beautiful, isn't it? That's the meaning of our lives—to be turned toward the Son of God! To be strengthened by his glory and guided by his grace. To hear his great love whispering in our ears.

Suddenly the shadows of fear fade, and the horizon of faith is limitless.

~

When the shadows of fear make us skittish, Lord, and rob
us of our faith, turn our face to the light of your great
love and power, and help us find our courage and
direction once again. In Christ, Amen.

The Voice of Encouragement

Read Acts 18:9-11

"Do not be afraid; keep on speaking."
—*Acts 18:9*

Martin Luther King, Jr., used to tell the story of an event that changed his life. On a Monday evening in 1956, he spoke at a church. Although he tried to appear strong and brave, in his heart he was afraid. The week before he had been arrested and thrown in jail for speaking the message of the gospel at a public gathering. Not only that, but he kept receiving telephone calls at home from people who called him a "dirty nigger" and threatened the lives of his wife and children.

So, when he spoke to the crowd that night, he wished he didn't have to be there; the fear in his soul made him tremble. But he thought he could hide his fear from the people, and when he finished speaking, he thought he had done quite well.

At the end of the service, though, an elderly woman called Mother Pollard came up to him. She said, "Something is wrong with you! You didn't talk strong tonight!"

King laughed a bit, nervous inside, and told her, "Oh, no, Mother Pollard. There's nothing wrong. I'm as fine as ever."

But she insisted. "Now, you can't fool me. I know something's wrong."

Before he could protest again, she said, "Dr. King, I done told you we is with you all the way." Then, said King, her face got bright, her voice grew quiet, and she said, "And even if we ain't with you, God's gonna take care of you."

"In that instant," King recalled, "I realized what was happening in my life. I was looking at the fears. I was looking at the doubts. I was looking at the terrors and the troubles that surrounded me.

"But old Mother Pollard made me see the most important thing in life. 'God's gonna take care of you!' she said." And for the rest of King's life, the voice of faith kept him going. Fear couldn't defeat faith.

In *Measure for Measure*, Shakespeare wrote, "Our doubts are traitors and make us lose the good we oft might win by fearing to attempt." As we come to our final reflections on doubt and faith, we know this is true.

Scripture's message is this: if life has thrown you down, and if fear would keep you on the ground, hear again the voice of Faith, the voice that says, "The Father loves you. No matter what may happen, Child, I'll never let go of your hand."

And when you hear that voice, get back into the saddle of your religion, the true religion of the Bible, and learn to ride on the winds of grace once more.

Love divine, all loves excelling,
Joy of heaven, to earth come down;
fix in us thy humble dwelling,
all thy faithful mercies crown.
Jesus, thou art all compassion,
pure, unbounded love thou art;
visit us with thy salvation,
enter every trembling heart.

Come, Almighty to deliver,
let us all thy life receive;
suddenly return, and never,
nevermore thy temples leave.
Thee we would be always blessing,
serve thee with thy hosts above,
pray and praise thee without ceasing,
glory in thy perfect love.

Finish, then, thy new creation;
pure and spotless let us be;
let us see thy great salvation
perfectly restored in thee:
changed from glory into glory,
till in heaven we take our place,
till we cast our crowns before thee,
lost in wonder, love, and praise. Amen!